WHSmith

Challenge

Maths

KS3: Year 7

Age 11–12

Hilary Koll and Steve Mills

Introduction

The *Challenge Maths* series will challenge and extend you in key maths topics in the curriculum at Key Stage 3.

The books are designed to be used throughout the year. Each double-page spread provides information about the nature of the topic, the key aspects that you are expected to master, and provides opportunities for you to practise and test your understanding. You will need to write your answers in a separate notebook.

Throughout the book are 'Try it yourself!' puzzles which encourage you to develop more effective thinking skills. These can be tackled independently of the rest of the page and can serve as a revision question when a topic is revisited.

By working through the *Challenge Maths* book, you will encounter the more difficult mathematics concepts appropriate for your year group and be encouraged to solve problems and puzzles requiring an advanced level of mathematical thinking.

First published 2007
exclusively for WHSmith by
Hodder Education, an
Hachette UK company,
338 Euston Road, London NW1 3BH

Impression number 10 9 8 7 6 5 4
Year 2011

A CIP record for this book is available from the British Library.

Cover illustration: Sally Newton Illustrations

Typeset by Servis Filmsetting Ltd, Manchester

ISBN 978 0 340 94554 4

Printed and bound in Spain.

Contents

1: Place value and decimals

You will revise:

- decimal notation and place value
- how to partition numbers.

Get started

It is important to know the value of each digit in a whole number or decimal.

Millions	Hundred thousands	Ten thousands	Thousands	Hundreds	Tens	Units	tenths	hundredths	thousandths
M	HTh	TTh	Th	H	T	U	t	h	th
	9	8	4	2	1	7	6	5	3

In the number 984 217.653:

- the digit 8 is worth 8 lots of ten thousand, which is 80 000
- the digit 5 is worth 5 hundredths, which is 0.05 or $\frac{5}{100}$
- the digit 3 is worth 3 thousandths, which is 0.003 or $\frac{3}{1000}$.

The number 984 217.653 can be partitioned into:

900 000 + 80 000 + 4000 + 200 + 10 + 7 + 0.6 + 0.05 + 0.003

Practice

1 The number 'ten thousand, one hundred and nine' in figures is 10 109. Write in figures these numbers written in words.

a six thousand, two hundred and forty-one

b thirty-one thousand and twenty-four

c one million, seven hundred and eleven thousand, six hundred and thirty-two

d two million, three hundred and nine thousand, and eighty

e sixty-two point nought nine six.

Challenge

2 Write the value of the digit in **bold type**. For example: in 0.6**3**4 the digit 3 is worth 0.03 or $\frac{3}{100}$; in 73**6**3.5 the digit 6 is worth 60.

a 3 **4**26 854 b 0.06**8** c 63 272.**6**37 d **8** 392 324.37

e 900 **8**31 f **84** 462.37 g 24.3**1**7

3 Partition these numbers.

a 17 070.2 b 8481.3 c 2.758

d 1 023 853.9 e 303 042.537

4 To change 368.69 to 368.79 you need to add 0.1. Write what must be added or subtracted to change:

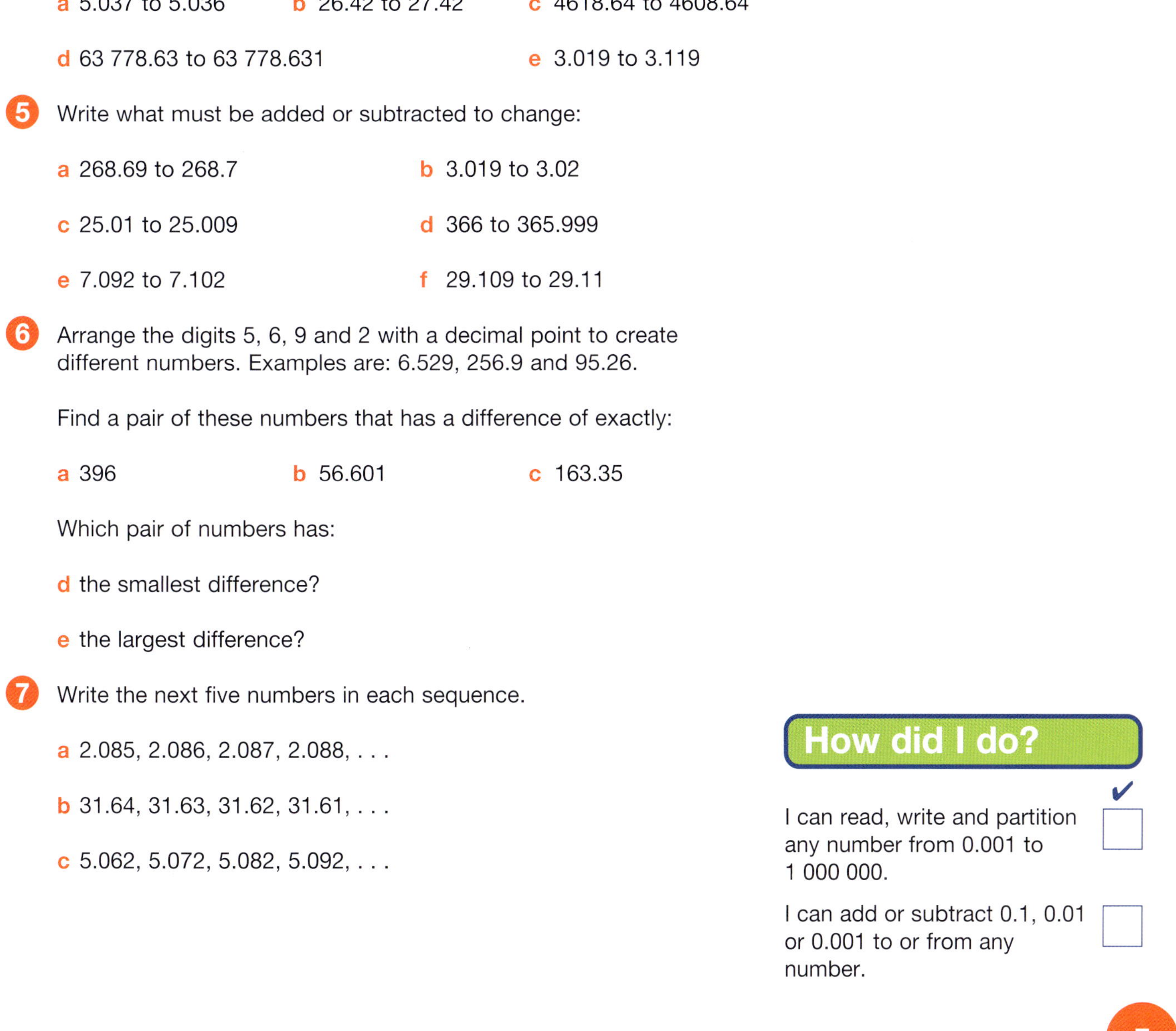

a 5.037 to 5.036 b 26.42 to 27.42 c 4618.64 to 4608.64

d 63 778.63 to 63 778.631 e 3.019 to 3.119

5 Write what must be added or subtracted to change:

a 268.69 to 268.7 b 3.019 to 3.02

c 25.01 to 25.009 d 366 to 365.999

e 7.092 to 7.102 f 29.109 to 29.11

6 Arrange the digits 5, 6, 9 and 2 with a decimal point to create different numbers. Examples are: 6.529, 256.9 and 95.26.

Find a pair of these numbers that has a difference of exactly:

a 396 b 56.601 c 163.35

Which pair of numbers has:

d the smallest difference?

e the largest difference?

7 Write the next five numbers in each sequence.

a 2.085, 2.086, 2.087, 2.088, . . .

b 31.64, 31.63, 31.62, 31.61, . . .

c 5.062, 5.072, 5.082, 5.092, . . .

How did I do?

	✔
I can read, write and partition any number from 0.001 to 1 000 000.	☐
I can add or subtract 0.1, 0.01 or 0.001 to or from any number.	☐

2: Fractions

You will revise:

- how to recognise and find equivalent fractions
- how to add and subtract fractions.

Get started

The **denominator** (bottom number) of a fraction shows how many equal parts the whole has been split into. The **numerator** (top number) shows how many of those equal parts are being described.

If two fractions have the *same denominator*, it is easy to add or subtract them.

- Add or subtract the numerators.
- Leave the denominators the same.

For example: $\frac{1}{7} + \frac{4}{7} = \frac{5}{7}$

To change a fraction to an equivalent one, multiply or divide the numerator *and* the denominator of the fraction by the same number.

Practice

1. Answer these questions. The fractions in each pair have the same denominator.

   a $\frac{3}{8} + \frac{1}{8}$ b $\frac{3}{9} + \frac{2}{9}$ c $\frac{3}{20} + \frac{12}{20}$ d $\frac{5}{6} - \frac{4}{6}$

   e $\frac{9}{10} - \frac{6}{10}$ f $\frac{3}{5} - \frac{1}{5}$ g $\frac{11}{12} - \frac{5}{12}$

2. Which of these additions and subtractions have an answer that is equivalent to $\frac{1}{2}$?

   A $\frac{3}{20} + \frac{7}{20}$ **B** $\frac{1}{6} + \frac{2}{6}$ **C** $\frac{3}{10} + \frac{2}{10}$ **D** $\frac{3}{8} + \frac{2}{8}$

   E $\frac{8}{11} - \frac{2}{11}$ **F** $\frac{10}{16} - \frac{2}{16}$ **G** $\frac{8}{10} - \frac{2}{10}$ **H** $\frac{17}{24} - \frac{5}{24}$

Challenge

3. Answer these questions, writing your answers as fractions.

   a Subtract one fifth from four fifths.

   b Write the fraction that is one seventh more than four sevenths.

   c Write the fraction that is one ninth less than six ninths.

   d Add three eighths and one eighth. Write your answer in its simplest form.

   e What is seven twelfths minus two twelfths?

4. Each of these is being rewritten so that the denominators are the same. Copy the sums and fill in the missing numerator to make an equivalent fraction and then answer the question:

a $\frac{3}{4} + \frac{1}{8} = \frac{\square}{8} + \frac{1}{8} =$

b $\frac{3}{5} + \frac{3}{10} = \frac{\square}{10} + \frac{3}{10} =$

c $\frac{7}{12} - \frac{1}{6} = \frac{7}{12} - \frac{\square}{12} =$

d $\frac{7}{9} - \frac{1}{3} = \frac{7}{9} - \frac{\square}{9} =$

5. A father decides to share some money between his three sons. He gives one third to his eldest son, and one ninth to his youngest son. The rest he gives to his middle son. What fraction of the money is the middle son given?

6. The Ancient Egyptians used only fractions with the numerator 1, called **unit fractions**, such as $\frac{1}{4}$, $\frac{1}{5}$ and $\frac{1}{8}$. To make other fractions they added different unit fractions. For example, $\frac{1}{2} + \frac{1}{3}$ is the same as $\frac{5}{6}$.

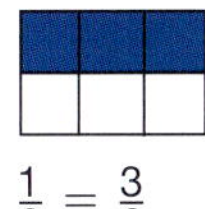

$\frac{1}{2} = \frac{3}{6}$

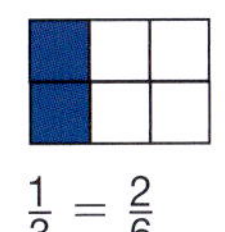

$\frac{1}{3} = \frac{2}{6}$

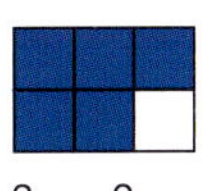

$\frac{3}{6} + \frac{2}{6} = \frac{5}{6}$

Which single fraction does each of these represent? Change fractions to equivalent ones to make the denominators the same in each question.

a $\frac{1}{2} + \frac{1}{4}$

b $\frac{1}{4} + \frac{1}{8}$

c $\frac{1}{5} + \frac{1}{15}$

d $\frac{1}{3} + \frac{1}{6}$

e $\frac{1}{2} + \frac{1}{4} + \frac{1}{8}$

f $\frac{1}{2} + \frac{1}{5} + \frac{1}{10}$

7. Arrange these fractions so that each row, diagonal and column has a total of $1\frac{1}{2}$. Remember that $1\frac{1}{2}$ is equivalent to $1\frac{5}{10}$ and $\frac{15}{10}$.

$\frac{2}{5}$ $\frac{1}{5}$ $\frac{1}{2}$ $\frac{3}{10}$ $\frac{3}{5}$

$\frac{1}{10}$ $\frac{4}{5}$ $\frac{7}{10}$ $\frac{9}{10}$

8. A farmer has a large flock of sheep of different breeds. One quarter of the flock is Suffolks, one fifth is Texels and one sixth is Jacobs. The rest of the flock is Oxfords. What fraction of the flock is Oxfords?

How did I do?

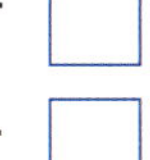

I know what a fraction means. ☐

I can find equivalent fractions. ☐

I can add and subtract fractions. ☐

3: Percentages

You will revise:

- how to calculate percentages of quantities.

Get started

A **percentage** is a fraction with a denominator of 100, but written in a different way.

'Per cent' means 'out of a hundred'. 36% means $\frac{36}{100}$.

To work out percentages in your head it can help to find these percentages first:

To find **50%**: halve the number.

To find **25%**: halve the number and halve the answer (or divide by 4).

To find **10%**: divide the number by 10.

To find **1%**: divide the number by 100.

Practice

1 Copy and complete these.

a 240

50% of 240 =

25% of 240 =

10% of 240 =

1% of 240 =

b 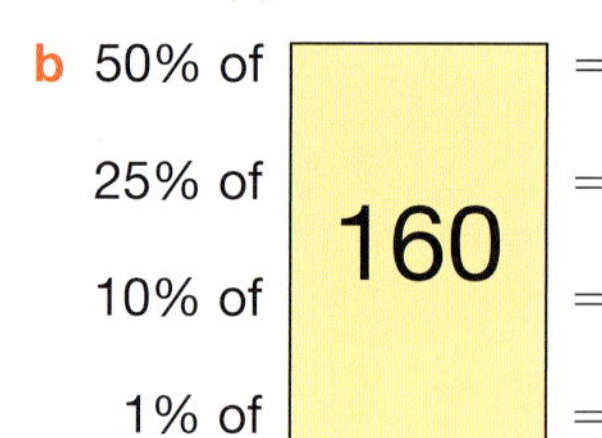

50% of 160 =

25% of 160 =

10% of 160 =

1% of 160 =

2 Work these out.

a 50% of £28 **b** 50% of 36 m **c** 25% of £88

d 25% of 600 g **e** 10% of 530 cm **f** 10% of 25 m

Challenge

3 Copy and complete these.

a 240

75% of 240 =

30% of 240 =

5% of 240 =

2% of 240 =

b 160

30% of 160 =

2% of 160 =

15% of 160 =

60% of 160 =

4 Answer these. Remember to write the unit of measurement each time.

a 30% of £120 b 2% of 300 m c 5% of £80

d 2% of 500 kg e 90% of 60 cm f 60% of 110 m

g 70% of 90 mm h 5% of 360 cm i 95% of 20 cm

5 Work these out without a calculator.

a In a sale you pay 70% of the original price. The original price for a shirt is £30. How much is the sale price?

b A woman who earns £24 000 in a year gives 5% of her earnings to charity. How much does she give each year?

c A baby girl weighs 90% of her expected weight. Her expected weight was 110 ounces. How much does she weigh?

6 a Find these percentages.

50% of 360
25% of 360
10% of 360
5% of 360
1% of 360
$\frac{1}{2}$% of 360

b Now use your answers to find these.

60% of 360	51% of 360
75% of 360	35% of 360
15% of 360	50.5% of 360
$25\frac{1}{2}$% of 360	16% of 360
11% of 360	66% of 360
6% of 360	$15\frac{1}{2}$% of 360

7 A worker is paid £55 a week day. If he works at the weekend he is paid 11% extra. How much does he earn if he works 7 days a week for:

a one week? b two weeks? c four weeks?

8 10% of £250 has an answer that is a whole number of pounds, £25.
a Which of these is a whole number of pounds?

1% of £250 2% of £250 3% of 250
4% of 250 5% of 250 6% of 250

b For £250, can you find a rule or rules that will tell you which percentages give whole-number answers?

How did I do?

I can calculate percentages of quantities.

4: Proportion

You will revise:

- what a 'proportion' is
- finding equivalent fractions, decimals and percentages.

Get started

When asked 'What proportion of a whole is something?' the answer could be given as a **fraction**, a **decimal** or a **percentage**. The proportion of sweets in a set that are red could perhaps be a quarter ($\frac{1}{4}$), 0.25 or 25%. Fractions, decimals and percentages are all used to describe parts of a whole.

This number line shows how some fractions, decimals and percentages are related.

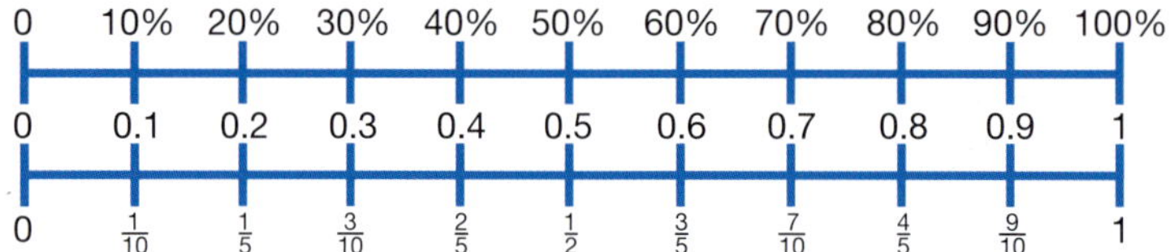

This diagram shows how to change fractions to decimals and then to percentages.
It also shows how whole-number percentages can be changed to fractions.

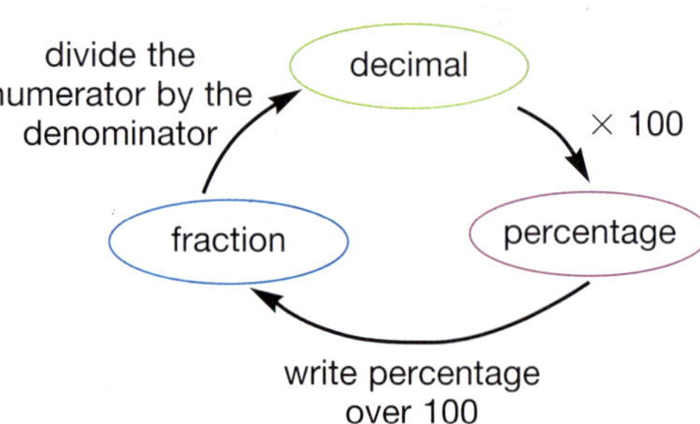

Practice

1 Write each fraction as a decimal and then as a percentage. You may use a calculator.

a $\frac{1}{2}$ **b** $\frac{1}{10}$ **c** $\frac{3}{10}$

d $\frac{7}{10}$ **e** $\frac{1}{4}$ **f** $\frac{3}{4}$

Challenge

2 Write each fraction as a decimal and then as a percentage. You may use a calculator.

a $\frac{6}{8}$ **b** $\frac{14}{20}$ **c** $\frac{3}{5}$

d $\frac{2}{5}$ **e** $\frac{4}{50}$ **f** $\frac{1}{8}$

3. Write each decimal as a percentage and then as a fraction. You may use a calculator.

a 0.34   b 0.98   c 0.27

d 0.03   e 0.4   f 0.7

4. Write each percentage as a fraction and then as a decimal.

a 64%   b 85%   c 16%

d 3%   e 70%   f 80%

5. What proportion of each shape is shaded? Give each answer as a fraction, as a decimal and as a percentage.

a

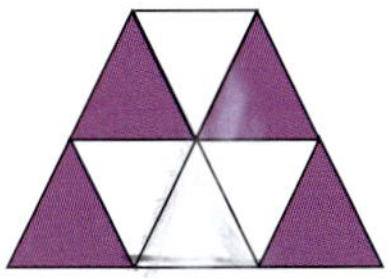

b

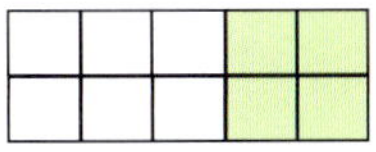

c

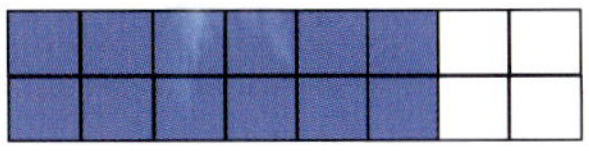

6. What proportion of each set is red? Give each answer as a fraction, as a decimal and as a percentage.

a 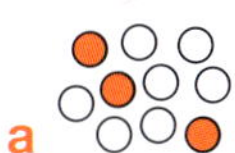

b 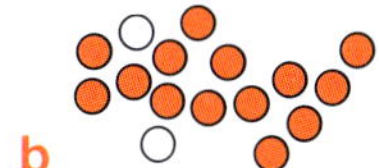

c 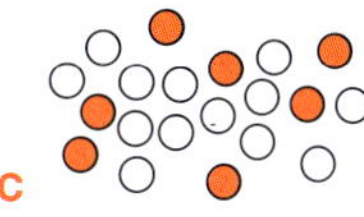

7. In a cinema the proportion of an audience that is female is 35%. What proportion is male? Give your answer as a decimal, as a percentage and as a fraction in its simplest form.

Try it yourself!

Arrange these digits and signs to make a fraction and an equivalent decimal and percentage.

       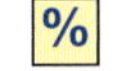

0 0 3 5 6 6 / . %

How did I do?

I understand what a 'proportion' is. 

I can find equivalent fractions, decimals and percentages. 

5: Ratio

You will revise:

- what a 'ratio' is
- how to simplify a ratio
- how to divide a quantity in a given ratio.

Get started

Ratio is the relationship between two or more numbers or quantities. It compares 'part with part'.

For this rod ▬▬▬□□, the *red parts* can be compared with the *white parts* and described as '3 red squares for every 2 white squares'. So the ratio of red to white is 3 to 2, written 3:2.

You can simplify a ratio by dividing the numbers in the ratio by the same number. When the numbers can no longer be divided to give whole numbers, the ratio is in its simplest form.

To divide an amount in a given ratio:

- first find out how many parts in the ratio there are altogether
- then divide the amount to find what 'one' part is worth
- then multiply to find 'many' parts.

Practice

1 Write each ratio in its simplest form.

a 9 : 12 b 16 : 32 c 36 : 4 d 14 : 21

e 6 : 8 f 10 : 25 g 24 : 16 : 12 h 27 : 54 : 18

2 In a safari park there are 5 lions, 25 giraffes and 30 baboons.

a What is the ratio of lions to giraffes? Give the ratio in its simplest form.

b What is the ratio of lions to baboons? Give the ratio in its simplest form.

c What is the ratio of giraffes to baboons? Give the ratio in its simplest form.

d What is the ratio of lions to giraffes to baboons? Give the ratio in its simplest form.

Challenge

3 Divide £63 in the ratio 2 : 5.

4 Divide £49 in the ratio 3 : 4.

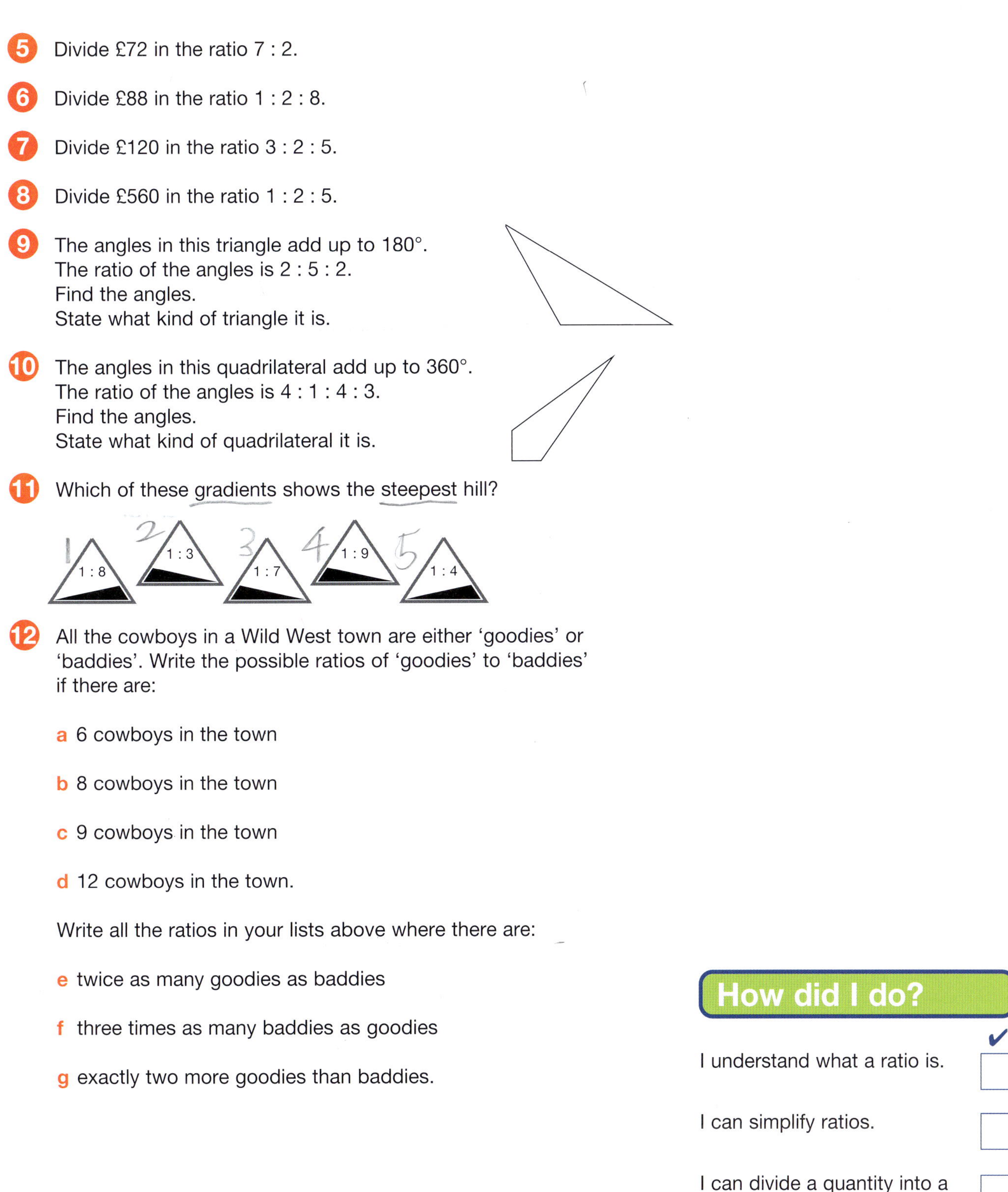

5 Divide £72 in the ratio 7 : 2.

6 Divide £88 in the ratio 1 : 2 : 8.

7 Divide £120 in the ratio 3 : 2 : 5.

8 Divide £560 in the ratio 1 : 2 : 5.

9 The angles in this triangle add up to 180°.
The ratio of the angles is 2 : 5 : 2.
Find the angles.
State what kind of triangle it is.

10 The angles in this quadrilateral add up to 360°.
The ratio of the angles is 4 : 1 : 4 : 3.
Find the angles.
State what kind of quadrilateral it is.

11 Which of these gradients shows the steepest hill?

12 All the cowboys in a Wild West town are either 'goodies' or 'baddies'. Write the possible ratios of 'goodies' to 'baddies' if there are:

a 6 cowboys in the town

b 8 cowboys in the town

c 9 cowboys in the town

d 12 cowboys in the town.

Write all the ratios in your lists above where there are:

e twice as many goodies as baddies

f three times as many baddies as goodies

g exactly two more goodies than baddies.

How did I do?

	✔
I understand what a ratio is.	☐
I can simplify ratios.	☐
I can divide a quantity into a given ratio.	☐

6: Positive and negative numbers

You will revise:

- how to add and subtract positive and negative numbers.

Get started

Positive and negative numbers can be shown on a number line.

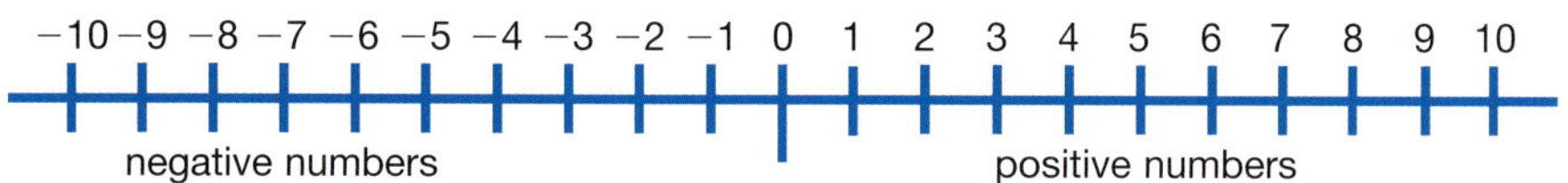

When *adding* numbers, count along the number line towards the *right*.

When *subtracting* numbers, count along the number line towards the *left*.

When two signs appear next to each other:

- think of $- -$ as a $+$, so $1 - -3 = 1 + 3$
- think of $+ -$ as a $-$, so $-3 + -4 = -3 - 4$.

Practice

1 Work out these additions, moving to the right on the number line.

a $-6 + 9$ **b** $-9 + 4$ **c** $-3 + 7$

d $-4 + 9$ **e** $-2 + 6$

2 Work out these subtractions, moving to the left on the number line.

a $-2 - 3$ **b** $5 - 8$ **c** $-4 - 8$

d $0 - 7$ **e** $-4 - 5$

Challenge

3 Work these out.

a $-5 + 9 =$ **b** $-7 - 2 =$ **c** $11 - 15 =$

$-5 - 9 =$ $7 - 2 =$ $-11 - 15 =$

$5 - 9 =$ $-7 + 2 =$ $-11 + 15 =$

4 Work these out.

a $-21 + 9$ **b** $-15 + 4$ **c** $-13 + 20$ **d** $-27 + 13$

e $-12 + 16$ **f** $-12 - 13$ **g** $21 - 28$ **h** $-24 - 8$

i $0 - 17$ **j** $-40 - 5$

5 Change each question to make it easier to answer, then answer it.
For example, $2 - -8 = 2 + 8 = 10$

a $-6 - -4$ **b** $-5 + -8$ **c** $5 + -9$ **d** $3 - -5$

e $-9 + -3$ **f** $15 - -11$ **g** $17 + -5$ **h** $-18 + -4$

6 In a quiz show, contestants score 2 points for a correct answer, -3 points for an incorrect answer and -1 point for a question not answered. What did each contestant score in total?

a not answered, correct, correct, incorrect, incorrect, correct, not answered

b correct, incorrect, correct, incorrect, correct, not answered, incorrect

c not answered, incorrect, correct, incorrect, correct, not answered, correct

d correct, correct, not answered, incorrect, incorrect, incorrect, correct, not answered

7 Here are five number cards.

-6	-9	8	4	-11

Which cards can be used to make each statement correct? Copy and complete them.

a $\square + \square = -2$ **b** $\square + \square = 2$

c $\square - \square = -2$ **d** $\square - \square = 2$

8 Copy and complete these magic squares so that each row, column and diagonal has the total shown.

a Total: 3

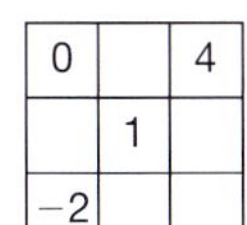

b Total: -3

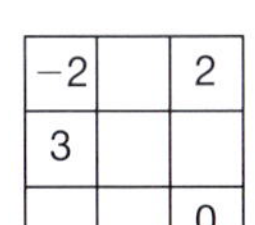

Try it yourself!

Copy and complete this magic square so that each row, column and diagonal has the total -9.

		0
	-3	-7
-6		

How did I do?

I can add and subtract positive and negative numbers.

7: Prime numbers, factors and multiples

You will revise:

- multiples, including common multiples
- factors, including common factors
- prime numbers.

Get started

A **multiple** is a number that is in a times table or beyond.
For example, multiples of 5 are 5, 10, 15, 20, 25, 30, . . . and carry on, such as 85, 115, 500 etc.

A number is a **common multiple** if it is a multiple of more than one number. For example, 21 is a common multiple of 3 and 7.

Factors are whole numbers that divide exactly into another number without a remainder. For example, the factors of 12 are 1, 2, 3, 4, 6 and 12 as they are the only whole numbers that divide exactly into 12 without a remainder.

A number is a **common factor** if it is a factor of more than one number. For example, 7 is a common factor of 14 and 21.

Prime numbers are whole numbers that have two factors, the number itself and 1. Examples are 2, 3, 5, 7, 11, 13, 17, 19, 23, 29, . . .

To find whether a number is a prime number, see how many factors it has. If it has exactly two factors, then it is prime. This means that the number 1 is not prime because it doesn't have two factors; its only factor is 1.

Practice

1 Copy and complete this multiplication grid.

×	1	2	3	4	5	6	7	8	9	10	11	12
3							21					
4												
5	5	10	15									
6												
7		14										
8												
9												

Challenge

2 Use your answers to the practice question to help you find the lowest common multiple of:

a 4 and 6 b 3 and 7 c 7 and 8 d 6 and 9

e 5 and 8 f 3, 6 and 9 g 3, 4 and 9 h 5, 4 and 6

3 Find all the factors of:

a 20 b 16 c 25 d 30 e 14

f 27 g 17 h 35 i 36 j 32

4 Which number in question 3 is prime?

5 Find four numbers between 10 and 30 that have exactly six factors.

6 Use your answers to question 3 to help you find the highest common factor of:

a 14 and 35 b 32 and 36 c 27 and 17

d 20 and 30 e 16 and 32 f 25 and 30

g 36 and 30 h 14 and 20 i 27 and 30

7 Find four numbers between 0 and 30 that have an odd number of factors. What is special about these numbers?

8 Here are some square numbers: 4, 9, 16, 25, 36, 49, 64, 81, 100.

Write each of these square numbers as the sum of two prime numbers. For example, $4 = 2 + 2$ (2 is prime).

a 9 b 16 c 25 d 36

e 49 f 64 g 81 h 100

9 Find out which number between 0 and 100 has:

a the fewest factors

b the most factors

c exactly 12 factors.

How did I do?

✔

I can find multiples and factors of a number. ☐

I can find common multiples and common factors of two numbers. ☐

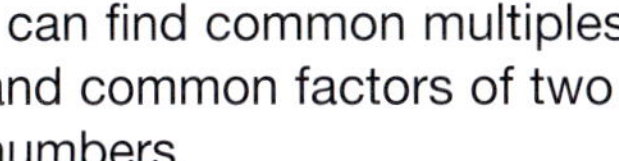

I can recognise prime numbers. ☐

8: Understanding number

You will revise:

- the order of operations when calculating.

Get started

There are four main **operations** in mathematics: adding, subtracting, multiplying and dividing.

Some questions involve more than one operation. Mathematicians have agreed on an order for doing calculations. The letters of **BODMAS** help you to remember the order of operations.

Do anything in **brackets** first.	**B**rackets
Next do **other** things such as squares, roots and powers.	**O**ther
Divide and **multiply** next.	**D**ivide
	Multiply
Finally **add** and **subtract**.	**A**dd
	Subtract

Practice

1 Without using a calculator copy and complete these.

a $36 \times \square = 0$	**b** $36 \times \square = 36$	**c** $36 + \square = 36$
d $\square \times 47 = 47$	**e** $47 - \square = 47$	**f** $47 \times \square = 0$
g $58 \div \square = 1$	**h** $58 \times \square = 0$	**i** $58 \div \square = 58$
j $\square + 95 = 95$	**k** $\square \times 95 = 95$	**l** $\square \div 95 = 0$

Challenge

2 Say whether each statement below is true or false.

a Adding zero to a number always gives the answer zero.

b Subtracting zero from a number always gives the number itself.

c Subtraction is the inverse (opposite) of addition.

d Division is the inverse of subtraction.

e Multiplication is the inverse of division.

f It doesn't matter which order you use to add numbers. The answer will always be the same.

Try it yourself!

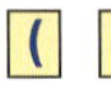

+ ×

Rearrange these cards to make questions with these answers. You do not need to use all the cards each time.

a 34	**b** 16
c 40	**d** 48

3 Work these out. Remember to use the order of BODMAS.

a $3 + 5 \times 6$ b $(6 + 9) \times 2$ c $16 \div 4 + 4$

d $20 - 16 \div 2$ e $21 \div 3 + 6$ f $14 \div (9 - 2)$

g $5 \times (4 - 2)$ h $(5 + 1)^2$ i $3 \times \sqrt{25}$

j $4 \times 2 + 5$ k $14 - 8 \div 2$ l $(15 - 6) \div 3$

m $(3 + 4) \times 5 + 1$ n $(4 + 6) \times (15 - 12)$ o $3 + 4^2$

4 Which of these have an answer of 16?

A [8] [+] [4] [×] [2] B [5] [+] [3] [×] [2] [+] [5] C [36] [÷] [(] [2] [+] [2] [)]

D [8] [+] [8] [÷] [2] [−] [1] E [20] [−] [(] [8] [−] [4] [)] F $\frac{6 \times 8}{6 - 3}$

5 A calculator has a broken key. The multiplication key [×] doesn't work. Write what you would key in to help you answer these questions. You do not have to find the answers.

For example, to find 175×2, key in $175 + 175$; to find 625×11, key in $6250 + 625$.

a 264×3 b 753×11

c $22 \times \square = 1034$ d 932×9

e $\square \times 72 = 2448$ f 36×101

g $367 \times 5 \times 2$ h 874×99

6 Say whether each statement below is true or false. Give three examples for each.

a Dividing zero by a number always gives the answer zero.

b Multiplying a number by zero always gives the answer zero.

c Dividing a number by one always gives the number itself.

d Multiplying a number by one always gives the answer one.

e Dividing by a positive whole number always gives a smaller answer.

f Multiplying by a positive whole number always gives a smaller answer.

How did I do?

I know and can use the correct order of operations when calculating.

9: Calculations

You will revise:

- mental and written calculation methods.

Get started

There are four main operations in mathematics: adding, subtracting, multiplying and dividing. Operations can be done mentally (in your head) or using pencil-and-paper methods.

Make sure you know number facts by heart, such as all the multiplication facts to 10×10 and related division facts. This will help you when calculating in your head and on paper.

You also need to learn to square numbers to 10 and to find the related square roots, such as $6^2 = 36$ and $\sqrt{36} = 6$.

Practice

1 Work out the correct answers for these questions.

$0 \div 6$	$42 \div 6$	$12 \div 6$	6×6	5×6
9×6	4×6	$18 \div 6$	10×6	$48 \div 6$
$0 \div 9$	9×9	$90 \div 9$	7×9	$45 \div 9$
6×9	4×9	$27 \div 9$	$18 \div 9$	8×9
$70 \div 7$	$21 \div 7$	$14 \div 7$	9×7	7×7
6×7	4×7	$35 \div 7$	8×7	$0 \div 7$
8×8	7×8	4×8	9×8	$16 \div 8$
6×8	$24 \div 8$	$40 \div 8$	$80 \div 8$	$8 \div 8$

Challenge

2 Answer these square and square root questions.

a 7^2 b $\sqrt{25}$ c 9^2 d $\sqrt{49}$

e 10^2 f 5^2 g $\sqrt{4}$ h 6^2

i $\sqrt{9}$ j 12^2 k $\sqrt{1}$ l 11^2

m $8^2 \div 4^2$ n $2^2 \times \sqrt{121}$ o $5^2 \div \sqrt{100}$

3 Copy and complete these patterns.

$0.1^2 = 0.1 \times 0.1 = 0.01$	$0.2^2 = 0.2 \times 0.2 = 0.04$
a $0.3^2 =$	b $0.4^2 =$
c $0.5^2 =$	d $0.6^2 =$
e $0.7^2 =$	f $0.8^2 =$
g $0.9^2 =$	h $1.0^2 =$
i $1.1^2 =$	j $1.2^2 =$

4 Use mental methods to answer these questions.

a A pen costs 68p. Ben buys two of them. How much change from £2 does he get?

b Li and Jo have 173p to share. What is the most they can each have if they each get the same amount?

c Two identical tickets cost £17.60 altogether. How much does one ticket cost?

d A TV costing £147 is reduced to half price in a sale. How much does it cost in the sale?

e Jo had £17.30 and bought a CD. She was left with £8.70. How much did the CD cost?

5 What number goes in each box?

a $0.65 + \square = 1$	b $55 + \square = 100$	c $2.5 + \square = 10$
d $45 + \square = 100$	e $\square + 8.5 = 10$	f $\square + 7.5 = 10$
g $\square + 65 = 100$	h $\square + 0.15 = 1$	i $10 - 6.3 = \square$
j $1 - 0.8 = \square$	k $1 - \square = 0.05$	l $100 - \square = 59$
m $0.64 + \square = 1$	n $56 + \square = 100$	o $2.7 + \square = 10$

6 Use written methods to answer these questions.

a $363 + 679$	b $519 + 648$	c $876 + 375$
d $6.594 + 4.069$	e $572 - 389$	f $1853 - 574$
g $9374 - 298$	h $767.53 - 352.91$	i 264×16
j 56×204	k 26.5×32	l 7.34×5.1
m $852 \div 4$	n $1035 \div 5$	o $184.8 \div 3$

Try it yourself!

Write any three consecutive numbers. Multiply the two outer numbers. Square the number in between. What do you notice about the two answers?

Try different sets of consecutive numbers. Does what you noticed always work?

What if you tried five consecutive numbers?

How did I do?

I can calculate mentally and using written methods.

10: Problem solving (1)

You will revise:

- how to solve word problems.

Get started

When faced with a problem to solve, follow these steps.

- Read the problem carefully.
- Look for any useful words in the question.
- Write down or circle any important numbers in the question.
- Decide what operations to use.
- Find an approximate answer.
- Decide whether to use a written or mental method and work it out.
- Finally check your answer.

Practice

1. Write whether you would use addition, subtraction, multiplication or division to answer these questions.

   a James is 42 years old and his daughter is half his age. How old is she?

   b Some children get into groups of 4. There are 8 groups. How many children are there?

   c My dad has eight sweets. He shares them between four of us. How many do we each get?

   d Fifteen people were on a bus. Eleven more got on. Now how many are on the bus?

   e Jane has 24 stickers. Pete has 8 fewer. How many stickers has Pete?

Challenge

2. Solve these word problems.

   a There are three times as many cars in a car park on Monday than on Sunday. 48 cars were parked there on Sunday. How many cars are there on Monday?

   b 9543 people visited the Coliseum cinema this year. This was 2704 more than last year. How many people visited the cinema last year?

   c Ella's mum is five times older than Ella. Ella's mum is 30. How old is Ella?

d There are 5 shelves. A supermarket has 20 tins of beans on each shelf. 32 tins get sold. How many tins are there now?

e A car park has 785 spaces of which 57 are empty. How many cars are in the car park?

f I had 49p. I was given 20p more. Then I spent 54p. How much do I have left?

g 25 cars are in the car park. 8 leave but 17 more arrive. How many cars are there now?

h Amy saves £1.50 of her pocket money each week. After 10 weeks she buys a CD costing £10. How much money does she have left after that?

i A teacher has 18 grey pencils and 15 coloured pencils. She gives away 6 pencils. How many pencils does she have in total now?

j My mum is four times older than me. She is 36. How old will I be in 5 years?

k My book has 48 pages. I have read 5 pages already. How many pages must I read to reach the middle of the book?

l Six apples cost 66p. How much does it cost to buy 4 apples?

m Jo buys a pencil costing 48p and a rubber costing 32p. How much less than £1 is this?

n A burger costs £2.20. Mr Wildman buys four burgers for his children. How much change does he get from £10?

o 46 eggs are put into boxes that each hold 6 eggs. How many boxes are needed? How many boxes will be full?

p A school has £62 to buy netballs. Each ball costs £4. How many can they buy?

q 45 children are going on a school trip. Each car can carry 4 children. How many cars will be needed?

r One CD and a magazine costs £19. Four CDs and a magazine costs £58. What is the cost of one CD?

s Which is greater: 25% of £5, or 75% of £1.60?

t The value of a £140 000 house increased by 14% in May and by a further 9% in July. What was its new value?

u In April, the cost of a new £125 tennis racket increased by 8%. Before the end of the season the new price was reduced by 15%. What was the end-of-season price?

Try it yourself!

Who earns more:

- a footballer who earns on average £1200 per day, or
- a supermodel who earns on average 77p per minute for every minute of the day?

How much do they each earn in a year?

How did I do?

I can solve word problems. ☐

11: Simplifying expressions

You will revise:

- how to simplify algebraic expressions by collecting like terms.

Get started

Simplifying means writing something more simply.

When simplifying expressions with letters and numbers, first count up how many of each letter there are, and then add up the constants (numbers on their own). This is called **collecting like terms**, grouping things that are the same together.

$a + b + 4 + 4b + 2a + a + 3$ First count the a's, then the b's, then the numbers

So $a + b + 4 + 4b + 2a + a + 3 = 4a + 5b + 7$

Practice

1 Simplify these expressions. For example, $g + 3g + h + h = 4g + 2h$.

a $m + m + 2n + n + 3m$

b $2c + 3d + c + 4c$

c $9e + f + f + f + 4e$

d $x + 5y + 5x + 2y$

e $7j + 3k + 2j + k + 2k$

f $a + 3a + b + c + 2b + 3c + a + 4a$

g $2p + 5q + q + r + 2r + p + p + 3q$

h $x + 4x + 2y + 3z + 2y + 5z + 6x + 4y$

i $2m + 4n + 3p + m + 2n + 5p + 3n$

Challenge

2 Simplify these expressions.

a $4a + 5b + 2a + 2b + 3b + 6 + 4 + 3$

b $4a + b + 5b + 4 + 3a + 5 + 2b + 2$

c $2a + 6b + 2a + 5a + 4b + b + 5 + 2$

d $10 + 2a + 5 + 5 + 3b + 5a + b + 1$

e $7a + 4b + 2b + 5 + 2a + 3 + 2a + 9$

3 Add the expressions in two bricks next to each other (the first one has been done for you). Simplify your answer and write it in the brick above. Keep going until you have finished the pyramid.

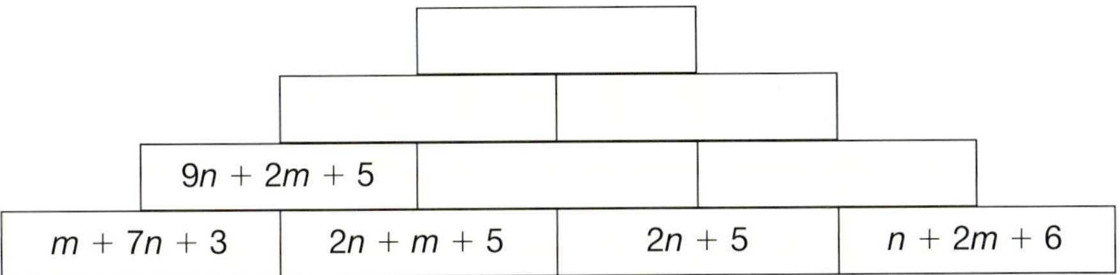

4 Simplify these expressions. Watch out for the negative signs.

a $2a + a + b + 7b - 2a$

b $8f + 2e + e - 5f + 4e + 1$

c $5i + h - 4i - h + 2h + 2$

d $t + 2t + 1 + 7u + t + 4u - 3$

e $2g + h + 5 + 4g - 6h - 1$

f $p - 2p + 8q + 3q - 8 + 5$

g $5y - y + 2x - y + x - 7 + 3$

h $4m + 2n + 7 - 5m - 5n + 6$

5

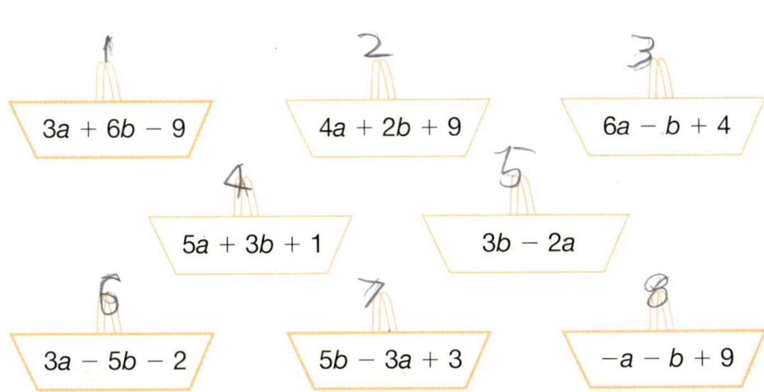

Choose any two baskets and add the expressions together, simplifying your answer.

Which two baskets have these totals?

a $a + 7b + 12$

b $9a - 6b + 2$

c $2a + 5b$

d $a - 2b - 2$

Try it yourself!

Write four expressions that could be simplified to the expression $5x + 2y - 1$.

How did I do?

I can simplify algebraic expressions by collecting like terms.

12: Linear equations

You will revise:

- how to construct and solve linear equations.

Get started

An **equation** always has an equals sign, as in $2y + 3 = 4y - 1$. What is on one side of the equals sign is worth the same as what is on the other side.

When there is only one unknown in an equation, it is possible to **solve** the equation. This means finding out what number the letter stands for.

Examples

I think of a number, add 9 to it and the answer is 15. What is my number?

Solution: Let my number be n. Then $n + 9 = 15$, so $n = 6$.

I think of a number, multiply it by 2 and add 9 to it and the answer is 15. What is my number?

Solution: Let my number be n. Then $2n + 9 = 15$, so $n = 3$.

Practice

1. Write an equation for each of these situations and find the unknown.

   a I think of a number, multiply it by 25 and the answer is 175. What is my number?

   b I think of a number, divide it by 6 and the answer is 12. What is my number?

   c I think of a number, subtract 12 from it and the answer is 79. What is my number?

   d I think of a number, add 36 to it and the answer is 78. What is my number?

   e I think of a number and subtract it from 20. I get 4. What is my number?

   Check each of your answers by putting the number back into the question.

Challenge

2. Write an equation for each of these situations and find the unknown.

   a I think of a number, multiply it by 2 and add 5. The answer is 75. What is my number?

b I think of a number, multiply it by 3 and add 1. The answer is 19. What is my number?

c I think of a number, multiply it by 5 and subtract 1. The answer is 39. What is my number?

d I think of a number, multiply it by 8 and subtract 7. The answer is 57. What is my number?

Check each of your answers by putting the number back into the question.

3 Solve these equations.

a $2a + 5 = 15$	**b** $7y - 3 = 32$	**c** $5f - 3 = 17$
d $3p + 7 = 22$	**e** $6d + 10 = 52$	**f** $4c - 4 = 28$
g $5b - 4 = 46$	**h** $3e + 6 = 21$	**i** $2a + 4 = 20$
j $3y + 17 = 26$	**k** $7f - 13 = 15$	**l** $4p + 4 = 16$
m $3d + 15 = 45$	**n** $4c - 6 = 26$	**o** $5b - 14 = 41$

4 The largest angle in this triangle is 100°. Find the value of n and use it to find the sizes of the other angles.

Check that the angles add up to 180°.

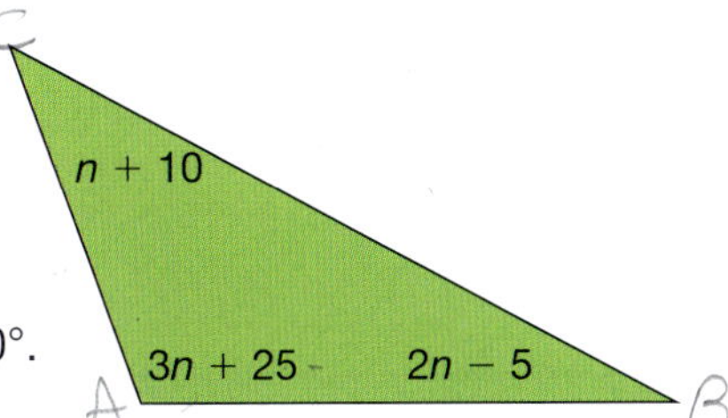

5 Find the value of x for each rectangle.

a

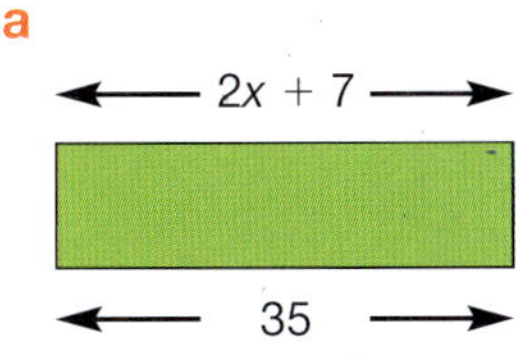

b

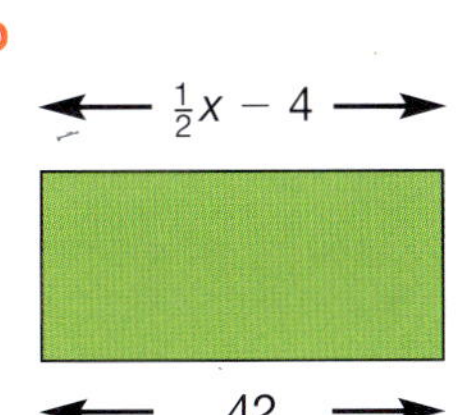

Try it yourself!

Ben and Ella got £44 between them for their birthdays. Ella got £8 more than Ben. How much did Ben get?

How did I do?

I can construct and solve linear equations. ✔ ☐

13: Formulae and substituting

You will revise:

- deriving and using formulae
- substituting values into a formula.

Get started

To **substitute** means to exchange (or replace) one thing for another. In sport, players are substituted. In maths, numbers are substituted for letters.

A **formula** is a way of writing a mathematical rule, showing the relationship between things. For example, this formula shows the relationship between the area of a rectangle and its length and width:

Area of a rectangle = length × width $\quad A = l \times w$

Values can be substituted into the formula to find an unknown.

Practice

1 A bookshop sells books costing £2 each. A formula for the cost (C) can be written as $C = 2n$, where n is the number of books bought.

Use the formula to find the cost C when:

a 3 books were bought, $n = 3$ **b** 4 books were bought, $n = 4$

c 8 books were bought, $n = 8$ **d** 11 books were bought, $n = 11$

e 9 books were bought, $n = 9$ **f** 15 books were bought, $n = 15$

Challenge

2 A theme park has an entrance fee of £5. Each ride at the fair costs £3. A formula for the cost (C) can be written as $C = 5 + 3n$, where n is the number of rides.

Use the formula to find the cost C when:

a $n = 3$ **b** $n = 4$ **c** $n = 7$ **d** $n = 6$

e $n = 5$ **f** $n = 10$ **g** $n = 8$ **h** $n = 12$

3 Substitute these values of y into $P = 6y + 1$ to find the value of P.

a $y = 3$ **b** $y = 4$ **c** $y = 10$

4 Substitute these values of m and n into $R = 10m - 2n$ to find the value of R.

a $m = 3$ and $n = 1$

b $m = 5$ and $n = 8$

c $m = 6$ and $n = 3$

d $m = 1$ and $n = 5$

5 The formula $P \approx L \div 4 \times 7$ can be used to convert (approximately) between litres and pints, where L is the number of litres and P is the number of pints.

Convert these amounts to pints using the formula $P \approx L \div 4 \times 7$.

a $L = 8$ litres

b $L = 12$ litres

c $L = 24$ litres

d $L = 28$ litres

e $L = 32$ litres

f $L = 44$ litres

g $L = 80$ litres

h $L = 100$ litres

i $L = 48$ litres

6 Use the formula $T = D \div S$ to calculate the time T (in seconds) it takes to travel a distance D (in metres) at a particular speed S (in m/s). You may use a calculator.

a $D = 722$ m, $S = 38$ m/s

b $D = 756$ m, $S = 42$ m/s

c $D = 840$ m, $S = 35$ m/s

d $D = 1014$ m, $S = 39$ m/s

e $D = 1645$ m, $S = 47$ m/s

7 Which of the following formulae gives the highest value of W when:

a $n = 2$

b $n = 3$

c $n = 4$

d $n = 5$

A $W = 2n + 1$

B $W = 12 - 2n$

C $W = 5n - 3$

D $W = \frac{1}{2}(n + 2)$

E $W = n^2$

F $W = 3(7 - n)$

G $W = 2(n + 4)$

8 This fence is made from identical planks of wood. Each fence post is one metre from the next.

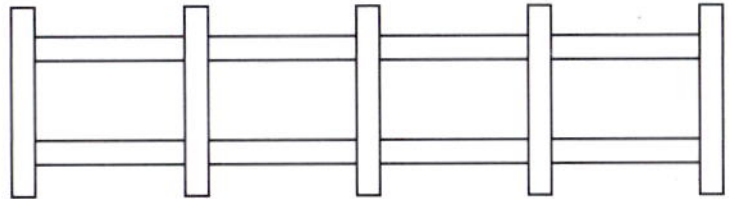

Write a formula for the number of planks P needed to make a fence that is N metres long.

Use this pattern to help you:

$N = 1, P = 4$

$N = 2, P = 7$

$N = 3, P = 10$

How did I do?

I can derive and use formulae from mathematics and other subjects. ☐

I can substitute values into a formula. ☐

14: Sequences

You will revise:

- how to generate sequences
- how to describe sequences using term-to-term and position-to-term rules.

Get started

Numbers arranged in a special order are called **sequences**. Each number in a sequence is called a **term**. There are two ways of describing sequences.

The **term-to-term rule** describes the first term and how each term is different from the previous term.

3, 7, 11, 15, 19, 23, . . .
The first term is 3. Each term increases by 4.

The **position-to-term rule** describes how to work out each term from where it is in the sequence, its position. For example, for this sequence, the position-to-term rule is: multiply the position number by 4 and subtract 1.

Position number	1	2	3	4	5	6
Term	3	7	11	15	19	23

Practice

1 Write the first eight terms of these sequences:

a The first term is 9. Each term increases by 2.

b The first term is 74. Each term decreases by 5.

c The first term is 127. Each term increases by 10.

d The first term is 1. Each term is multiplied by 2.

e The first term is 512. Each term is divided by 2.

Challenge

2 Describe each sequence using the term-to-term rule.

a 5, 8, 11, 14, 17, 20, . . .

The first term is ______. Each term is ______ by ______.

b 77, 72, 67, 62, 57, 52, . . .

c 10, 7.5, 5, 2.5, 0, −2.5, . . .

d 0.8, 0.6, 0.4, 0.2, 0, −0.2, . . .

3 Write the first eight terms of these sequences:

a The first term is 0. Each term increases by 0.25.

b The first term is 17.5. Each term decreases by 0.5.

c The first term is 12.7. Each term increases by 0.1.

d The first term is 6.25. Each term decreases by 0.1.

e The first term is 8.4. Each term increases by 0.5.

4 Write the first five terms of these sequences.

a Multiply the position number by 6 and add 1.

b Multiply the position number by 4 and subtract 2.

5 Write the term-to-term and the position-to-term rule for each of these sequences. One has been done for you as an example.

Position number	1	2	3	4	5	6
Term	4	8	12	16	20	24

Term-to-term rule: First term is 4. Add 4 each time.
Position-to-term rule: Multiply the position number by 4.

a

Position number	1	2	3	4	5	6
Term	7	14	21	28	35	42

b

Position number	1	2	3	4	5	6
Term	6	11	16	21	26	31

6 Write a sequence to match each of these descriptions. Then state the term-to-term rule and the position-to-term rule.

a Each term is a multiple of 5.

b Each term is an even number.

c Each term ends with the digit 3.

How did I do?

I can generate sequences. ☐

I can describe sequences using term-to-term and position-to-term rules. ☐

15: Problem solving (2)

You will revise:

- how to solve problems by first writing a formula.

Get started

Some problems can be solved by writing a formula and substituting values into it. It can help to write the formula in words first and then write it using just symbols, like this:

The length of P is four times the length of R. So $P = 4R$.

Practice

1 The length of a line AB is x cm. The line CD is three times the length of AB. A third line EF is 1 cm longer than CD.

A —— B (x)

C —————— D

E ———————— F

a Express the length of line CD in terms of x.

b Express the length of line EF in terms of x.

c Find the length of CD if line AB is 5 cm long.

d Find the length of EF if line AB is 7 cm long.

Challenge

2 A badge is made from two identical equilateral triangles as shown below. Some of the lengths are shown.

a Write a formula for x in terms of d.

b Express the perimeter P of the badge in terms of d.

c Find the length of x if $d = 4$ cm.

d Find the perimeter P of the badge if $d = 4$ cm.

e Find the value of d if the perimeter of the badge is 90 cm.

3 Point C is the centre of a circle with radius, r. The circle passes through the centre of the square ABCD. d is the shortest distance between the edge of the circle and point D.

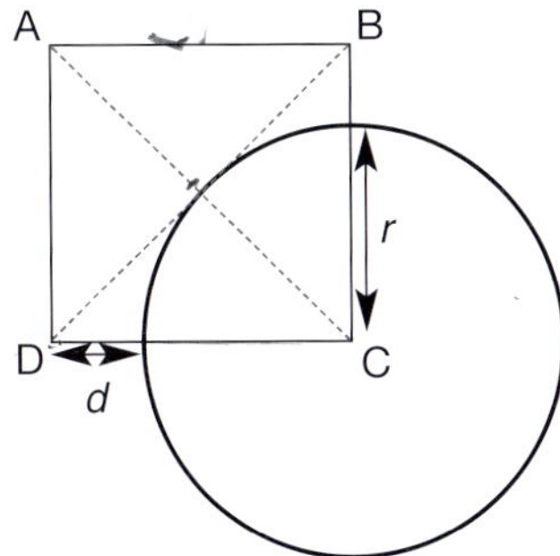

a Express the length of the diagonal AC in terms of r.

b Express the length of the side AB in terms of d and r.

c Express the perimeter P of the square ABCD in terms of d and r.

d Express the area of the square ABCD in terms of d and r.

4 Use your answers above to find the following measurements if $d = 4.1$ cm and $r = 10$ cm.

a The length of the diagonal AC.

b The length of the side AB.

c The perimeter P of the square ABCD.

d The area of the square ABCD.

5 The perimeter of a rectangle is 48 cm. Its area is 128 cm^2. What is the length and width of the rectangle?

$2l + 2w = 48$ cm

$2(l + w) = 48$ cm

$l + w = 24$ cm

$l \times w = 128$ cm^2

How did I do?

I can solve problems by using formulae. ☐

16: Angles

You will revise:

- the sum of angles on a straight line, inside a triangle and around a point
- using these facts to solve problems.

Get started

Angles on a straight line add up to 180°.

Angles inside a triangle add up to 180°.

Angles around a point add up to 360°.

Practice

1 Calculate the size of each of the marked angles.

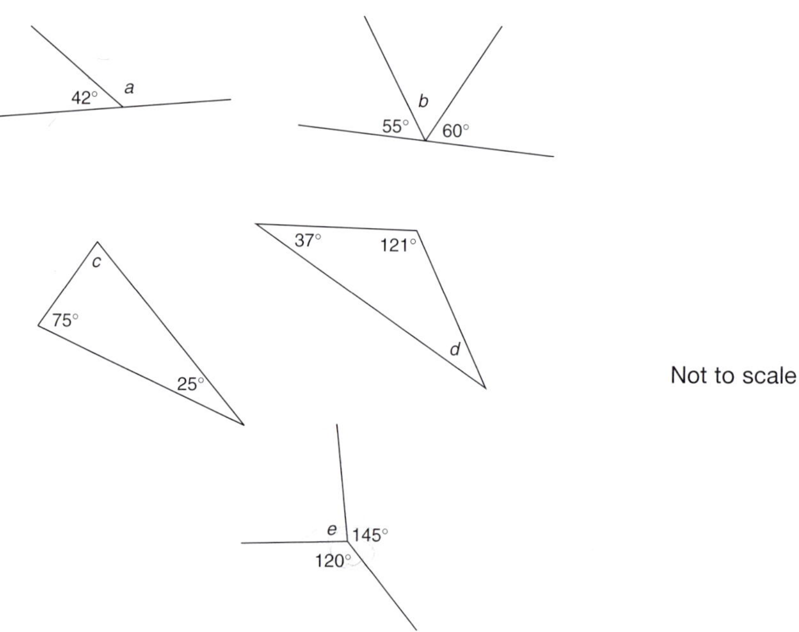

Not to scale

Challenge

2 Find the missing angles *a*, *b* and *c*.

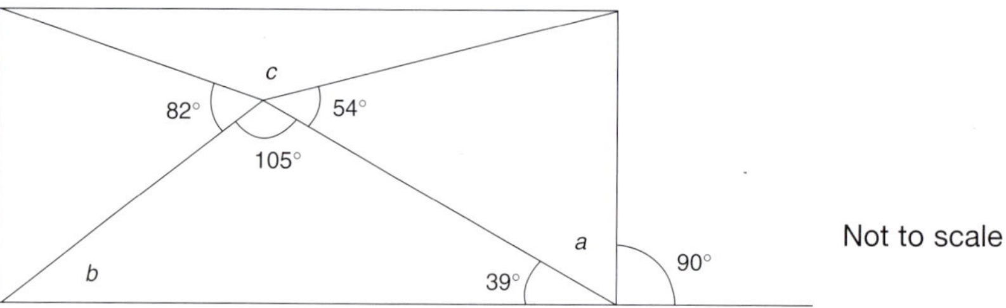

Not to scale

3 Find the missing angles *d*, *e* and *f*.

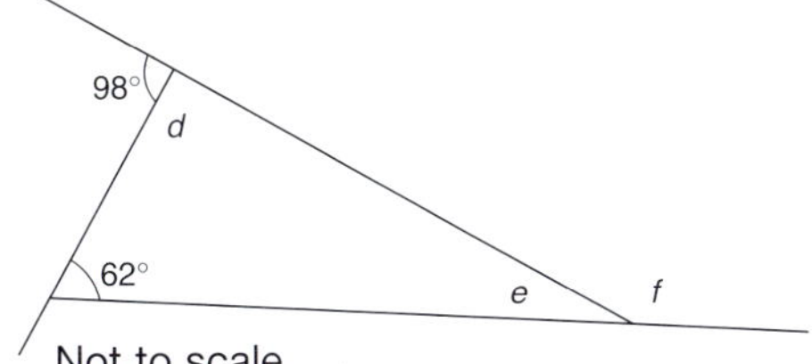

4 Find the missing angles *g*, *h*, *i*, *j* and *k*.

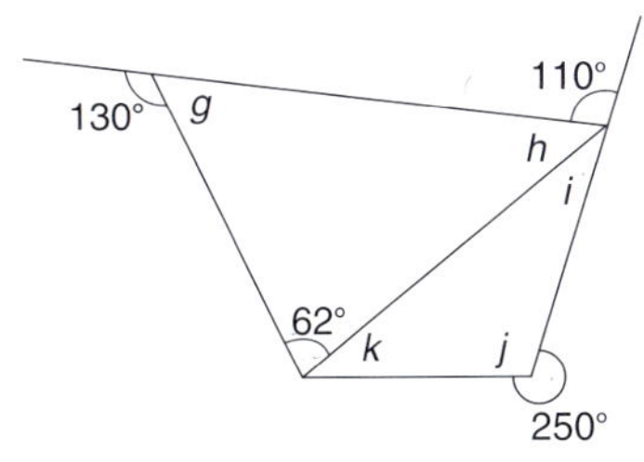

Not to scale

5 Find the missing angles *a*, *b* and *c*.

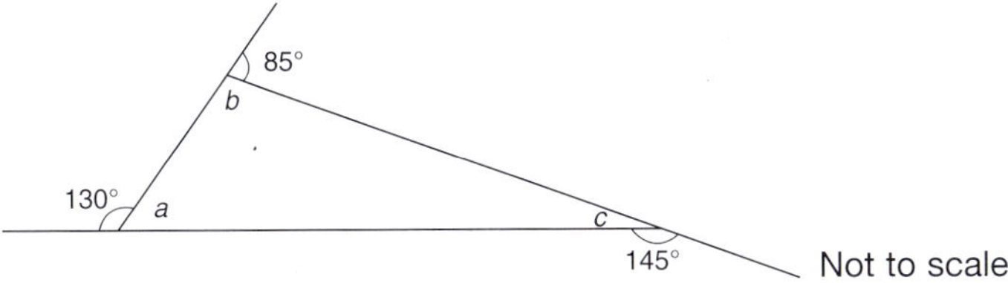

Not to scale

6 Use the answers to question 5 to help you fill in these angles:

a Angle *a* + angle *b* = ________

b Angle *b* + angle *c* = ________

c Angle *c* + angle *a* = ________

What do you notice about the sum of two of the interior angles and the opposite exterior angle?

Try it yourself!

Find the missing angles in this diagram. Explain how you worked them out.

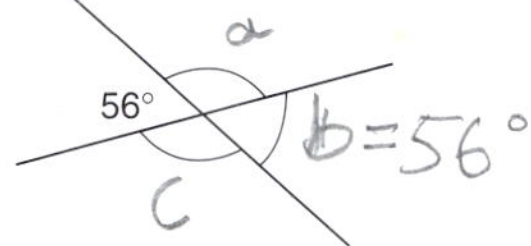

How did I do?

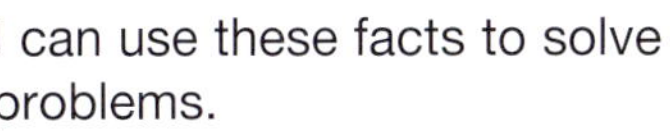

I know the sum of angles on a straight line, inside a triangle and around a point. ☐

I can use these facts to solve problems. ☐

17: Coordinates

You will revise:

- reading and plotting points using coordinates in all four quadrants.

Get started

The **origin** is the point (0, 0) on a coordinate grid.

Coordinates are written as pairs of numbers inside brackets, like (3, 2). The first number (the ***x*-coordinate**) tells you how many across from the origin to move and the second number (the ***y*-coordinate**) tells you how many up or down from the origin to move.

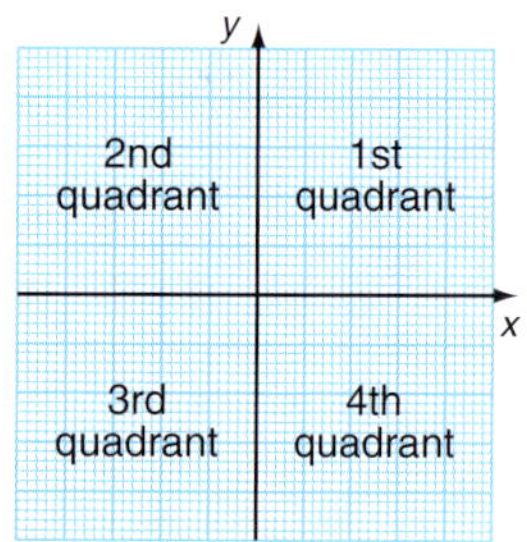

(4, −3) means start at the origin and move 4 to the right and 3 down.

(−4, −3) means start at the origin and move 4 to the left and 3 down.

(−4, 3) means start at the origin and move 4 to the left and 3 up.

Practice

1. Write the coordinates of points A, B, C and D.

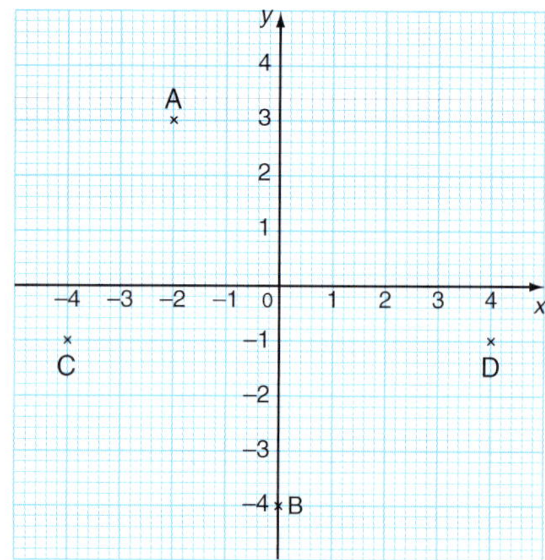

2. Copy the axes and points A, B, C, D above and plot and label these new points:

E (−3, 1) F (2, 0) G (−2, −2) H (−1, 4)

Challenge

3 Follow these instructions. Use the grid you have drawn.

a Join points C and E with a straight line.
Join points C and G with a straight line.
Points E, C and G are three vertices of a square.
What are the coordinates of the fourth vertex?

b Join points A and H with a straight line.
Join points H and D with a straight line.
Points A, H and D are three vertices of a rectangle.
What are the coordinates of the fourth vertex?

c Join points G and F with a straight line.
Join points F and D with a straight line.
Points G, F and D are three vertices of a parallelogram.
What are the coordinates of the fourth vertex?

4 Three vertices of a rectangle are at (0, −2), (5, −2) and (0, −3).
What are the coordinates of the fourth vertex?

5 Three vertices of a rectangle are at (−3, −2), (−1, −2) and (−3, 6).
What are the coordinates of the fourth vertex?

6 A square has opposite vertices at (3, 3) and (0, 0).
What are the coordinates of the other two vertices?

7 A square has opposite vertices at (2, −2) and (0, 0).
What are the coordinates of the other two vertices?

8 A square has opposite vertices at (−3, −4) and (−1, −2).
What are the coordinates of the other two vertices?

9 All but one of these points lie along a straight line. Which is the odd one out?

A (2, 4) **B** (−1, −2) **C** (1, 2) **D** (0, 0)

E (−2, −4) **F** (−4, −2) **G** (3, 6)

10 All but one of these points lie along a straight line. Which is the odd one out?

A (2, −1) **B** (−1, 2) **C** (−2, 3) **D** (1, 0)

E (0, 1) **F** (−3, −4) **G** (4, −3)

Try it yourself!

A hexagon has vertices at (0, 1), (2, −2), (−1, −4), (−2, −3), (−3, −3) and (−3, −1). How many right angles has this hexagon?

How did I do?

	✔
I can read and plot points using coordinates in all four quadrants.	☐
I can plot points determined by geometric information.	☐

18: Constructing triangles

You will revise:

- using a ruler and protractor to construct triangles from given information.

Get started

You will need a protractor, a ruler and a sharp pencil.

Protractors are used to measure and draw angles. They can be semicircular or circular.

When drawing angles, make sure the central cross of the protractor is at the end of the line where the angle will be and that the line matches up with the zero line on the protractor.

Practice

1 Here is a triangle ABC.

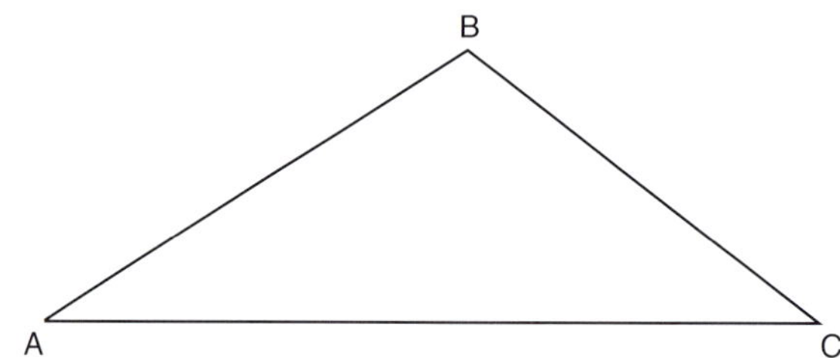

a Use a ruler to measure side AC in centimetres.

b Use a protractor to measure angle A.

c Use a ruler to measure side AB in centimetres.

Challenge

2 Use a ruler and protractor to construct triangle ABC with:

side AC = 5 cm, angle A = 58°, side AB = 4 cm

Now measure the length of side BC.

3 Use a ruler and protractor to construct triangle ABC with:

side AC = 4.2 cm, angle A = 23°, side AB = 4.3 cm

Now measure the length of side BC.

4 Here is a triangle ABC.

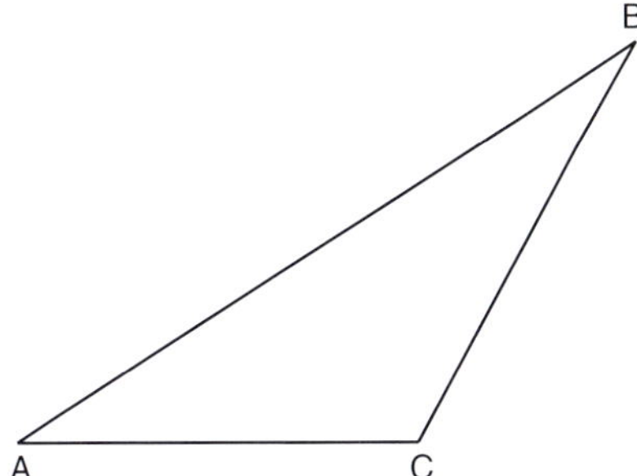

a Use a protractor to measure angle A.

b Use a ruler to measure side AC in centimetres.

c Use a protractor to measure angle C.

5 Use a ruler and a protractor to construct triangle ABC with:

angle A = 44°, side AC = 7 cm, angle C = 67°

a Measure angle B.

b Measure the length of side AB.

c Measure the length of side BC.

6 Use a ruler and a protractor to construct a triangle ABC with:

angle A = 24°, side AC = 6.6 cm, angle C = 98°

a Measure angle B.

b Measure the length of side AB.

c Measure the length of side BC.

7 Match these triangles to their correct descriptions.

Triangle 1: angle A = 30°, angle B = 60°, angle C = 90°

Triangle 2: angle A = 30°, angle B = 80°, angle C = 70°

Triangle 3: angle A = 110°, side AB = side AC

scalene triangle

obtuse isosceles triangle

right-angled scalene triangle

How did I do?

I can use a ruler and protractor to construct triangles from given information.

19: Perimeter and area

You will revise:

- the perimeter and area of shapes
- how to find the perimeter and area of a shape, including using formulae.

Get started

Perimeter is the distance around the edge of a shape. It is measured in units of length such as centimetres (cm) or metres (m).

The perimeter P of a rectangle of length l and width w can be found using the formula $P = 2(l + w)$.

Area is the amount of surface that a shape covers. It is the space inside the outline of a 2-D shape or within a boundary. Area is measured in square units such as square centimetres (cm^2) or square metres (m^2).

The area A of a rectangle can be found using the formula $A = l \times w$.

Practice

1 Find the perimeter and area of this rectangle. Give the correct unit of measurement.

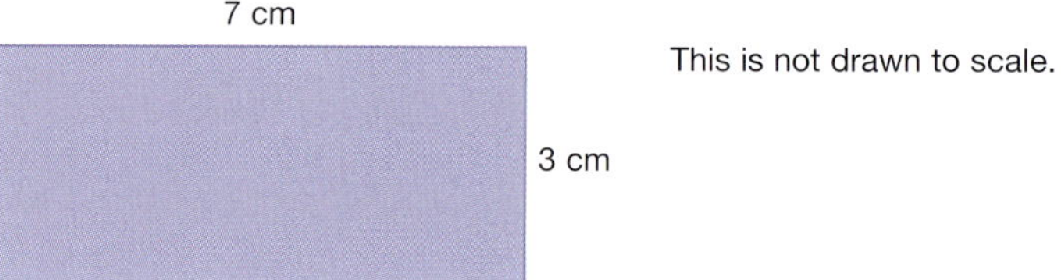

2 Find the perimeter and area of this rectangle. Give the correct unit of measurement.

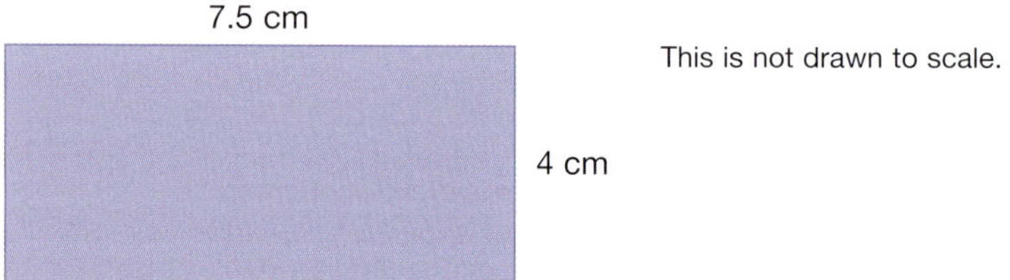

Challenge

3 Find the perimeter and area of each shape by splitting it into rectangles, giving the correct unit of measurement.

a

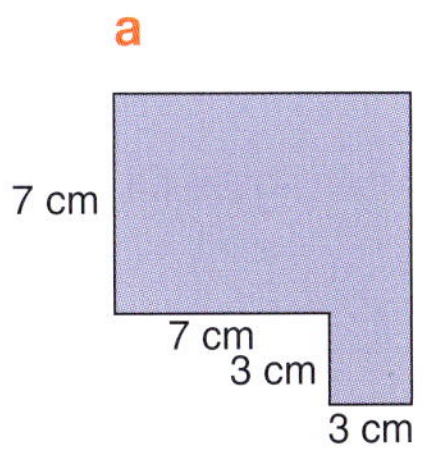

b

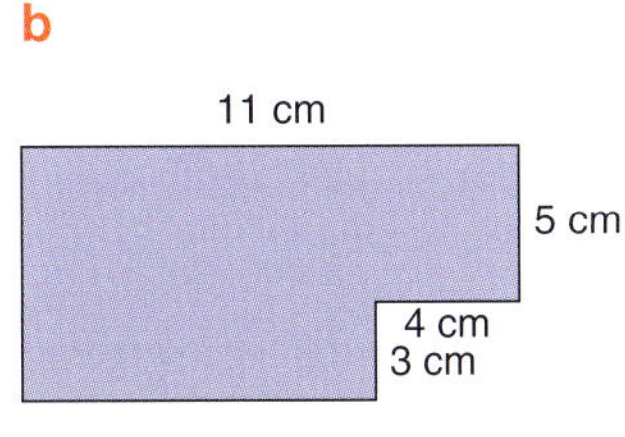

c

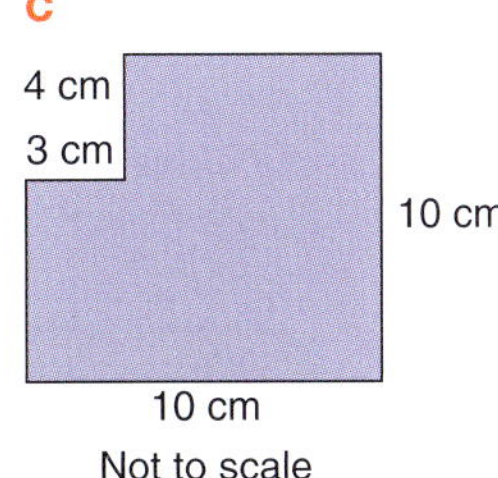

Not to scale

4 Find the perimeter and area of each shape by splitting it into rectangles, giving the correct unit of measurement.

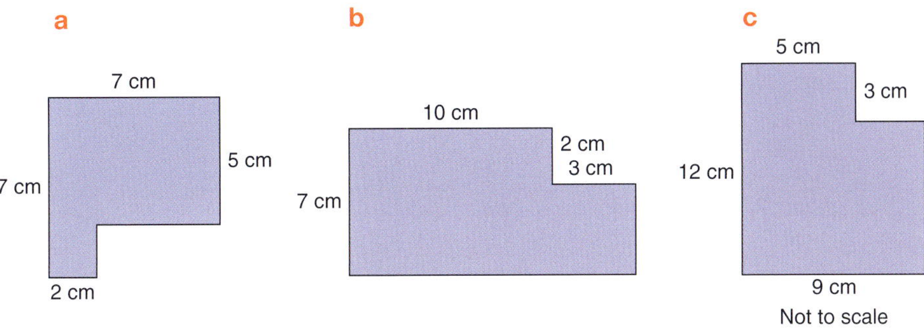

Not to scale

5 Find the perimeter and area of each shape by splitting it into rectangles, giving the correct unit of measurement.

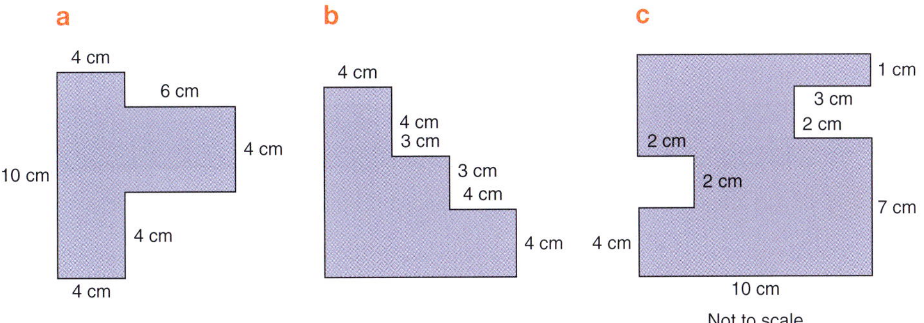

Not to scale

Try it yourself!

A rectangle has an area of 48 cm^2. Its length is 2 cm longer than its width. What is the perimeter of the rectangle?

How did I do?

I can find the perimeter and area of a shape, including using formulae.

20: Surface area

You will revise:

- how to find the surface area of a cuboid.

Get started

Area is the amount of surface that a shape covers. In a 2-D shape (flat shape) it is the space inside the lines or within a boundary. In a 3-D shape (solid shape) it is the total amount of surface of all the faces. For 3-D shapes this is often called the **surface area**.

Surface area is measured in square units such as square centimetres (cm^2) or square metres (m^2).

Practice

1 Find the missing dimensions on the net of this cuboid.

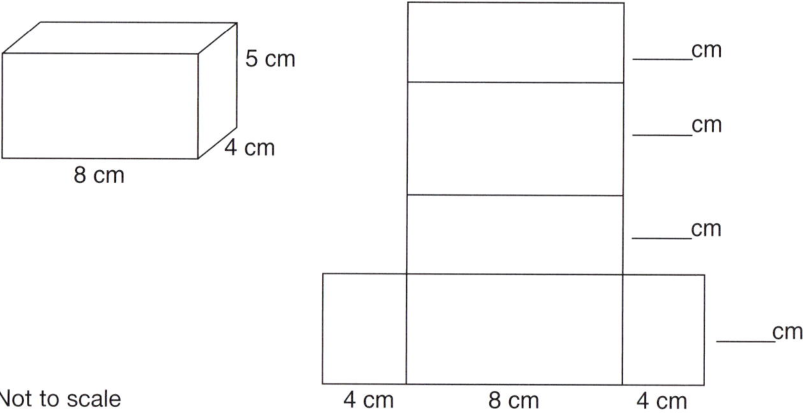

Not to scale

Work out the area of each rectangle of the net and use your answers to find the cuboid's surface area.

Challenge

2 Find the surface area of this cuboid. Sketch a net to help you.

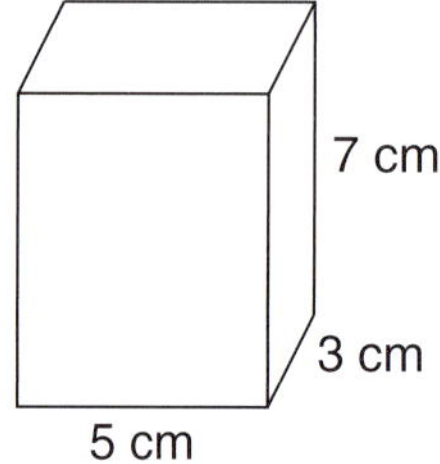

Not to scale

3 Find the surface area of this cuboid. Sketch a net to help you.

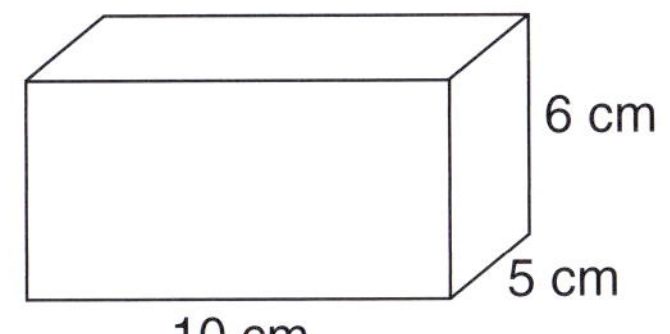

Not to scale

4 The formula for the surface area S of a cuboid with length l, breadth b and height h is:

$S = 2bl + 2lh + 2hb$

Find the surface area for a cuboid with these dimensions.

a $l = 7$ cm, $b = 5$ cm, $h = 12$ cm **b** $l = 9$ cm, $b = 4$ cm, $h = 6$ cm

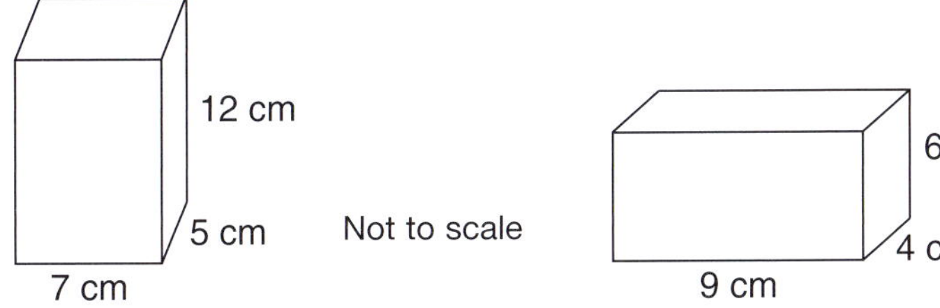

c $l = 4$ cm, $b = 2$ cm, $h = 8$ cm **d** $l = 15$ cm, $b = 7$ cm, $h = 6$ cm

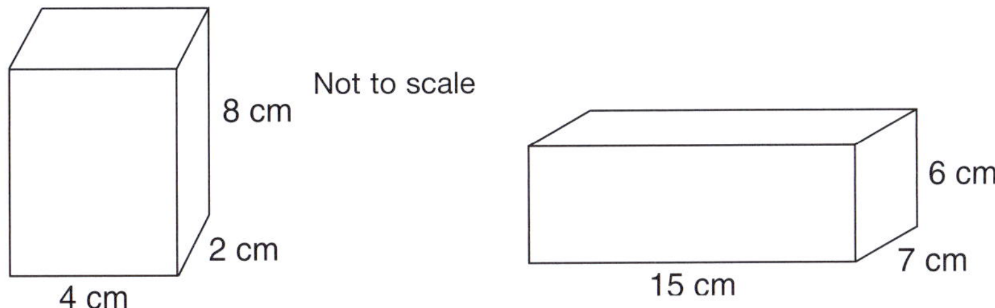

5 A cuboid has a length of 6 cm and a width of 4 cm. What is its height if its surface area is 148 cm^2?

How did I do?

I can find the surface area of a cuboid. ✔ ☐

21: Measurement

You will revise:

- standard metric units for length, mass and capacity
- converting between metric units.

Get started

These diagrams show how to convert from one metric unit to another.

mm ↔ cm	cm ↔ m	m ↔ km	g ↔ kg	ml ↔ l
10 mm = 1 cm	100 cm = 1 m	1000 m = 1 km	1000 g = 1 kg	1000 ml = 1 l

	mm → cm	cm → m	m → km	g → kg	ml → l
Smaller to larger unit	÷ 10	÷ 100	÷ 1000	÷ 1000	÷ 1000
Larger to smaller unit	× 10	× 100	× 1000	× 1000	× 1000

Practice

1 Convert these measurements to the units shown.

a 30 cm = □ mm

b 300 cm = □ m

c 60 mm = □ cm

d 470 mm = □ cm

e 9000 m = □ km

f 20 000 m = □ km

g 5000 mm = □ cm

h 700 cm = □ mm

i 6 m = □ cm

j 400 cm = □ mm

k 8000 m = □ km

l 700 m = □ cm

Challenge

2 Convert these measurements to the units shown.

a 1000 g = □ kg

b 7000 g = □ kg

c 4500 g = □ kg

d 8 kg = □ g

e 3.5 kg = □ g

f 5.7 kg = □ g

g 1.5 l = □ ml

h 2500 ml = □ l

i 16.8 l = □ ml

3 Convert these measurements to the units shown.

a 37 cm = ☐ mm b 128 cm = ☐ m c 67 mm = ☐ cm

d 473 mm = ☐ cm e 986 m = ☐ km f 2380 m = ☐ km

g 4902 m = ☐ km h 354 m = ☐ km i 0.78 m = ☐ cm

4 Convert these measurements to the units shown.

a 1200 g = ☐ kg b 1640 g = ☐ kg c 4362 g = ☐ kg

d 866 g = ☐ kg e 3.5 kg = ☐ g f 5.33 kg = ☐ g

g 1.584 l = ☐ ml h 1647 ml = ☐ l i 16.67 l = ☐ ml

5 Convert these measurements to the units shown.

a 150 mm = ☐ m b 1000 mm = ☐ m c 2500 cm = ☐ km

d 362 mm = ☐ m e 1387 cm = ☐ km f 0.56 m = ☐ mm

g 1560 mm = ☐ m h 8900 cm = ☐ km i 5660 mm = ☐ m

j 8092 mm = ☐ m k 867 cm = ☐ km l 0.819 km = ☐ cm

6 Write whether each statement is true or false:

a 0.007 mm = 7 m b 7 mm = 0.007 m

c 65 cm = 6 500 000 km d 6 500 000 cm = 65 km

e 800 000 mm = 800 m f 800 mm = 800 000 m

g 42 cm = 0.00042 km h 0.000 42 cm = 42 km

7 Arrange these cards to make at least five different pairs of equal measurements. You do not have to use all the cards each time.

[km] [m] [cm] [mm] [6] [6] [4] [4] [0] [0] [0] [0]

[.] [.] [=]

How did I do?

	✓
I know the standard metric units for length, mass and capacity.	☐
I can convert between metric units.	☐

22: Problem solving (3)

You will revise:

- how to investigate and solve shape and space problems.

Get started

When solving problems or investigating mathematical situations, it is often easier to break the problem down into smaller steps and then to look for patterns. Breaking it into smaller steps might mean starting with a smaller number and working your way up systematically. Drawing and completing a table can also help you to analyse the information more clearly.

Practice

1 This design has three different-sized squares: small, medium and the large square itself. Find the total number of squares in the design.

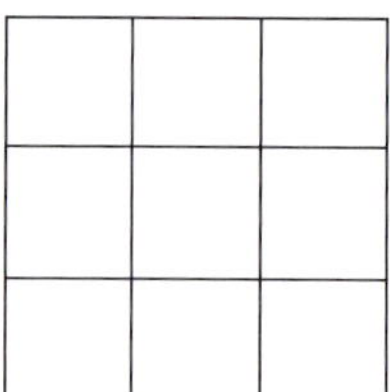

2 This design has three different-sized triangles: small, medium and the large triangle itself. Find the total number of triangles in the design.

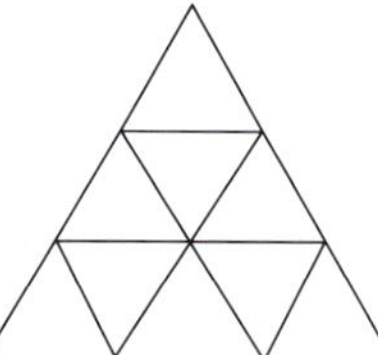

Challenge

3 You can split a square into 3 regions using 2 straight lines, like this:

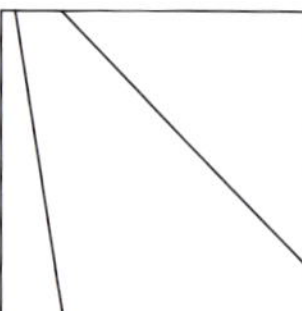

Or you can use 2 straight lines to split the square into 4 regions, like this:

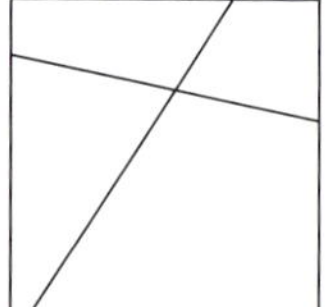

Find the smallest number of straight lines needed to create:

a 6 regions

b 9 regions

c Copy and complete this table.

Number of lines	0	1	2	3	4	5	6
Maximum number of regions							

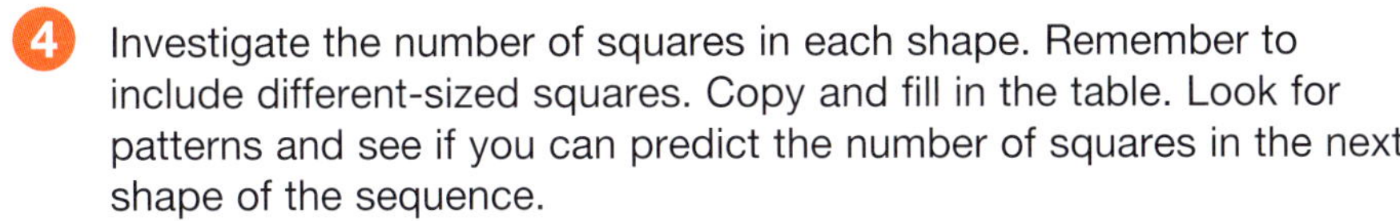

4 Investigate the number of squares in each shape. Remember to include different-sized squares. Copy and fill in the table. Look for patterns and see if you can predict the number of squares in the next shape of the sequence.

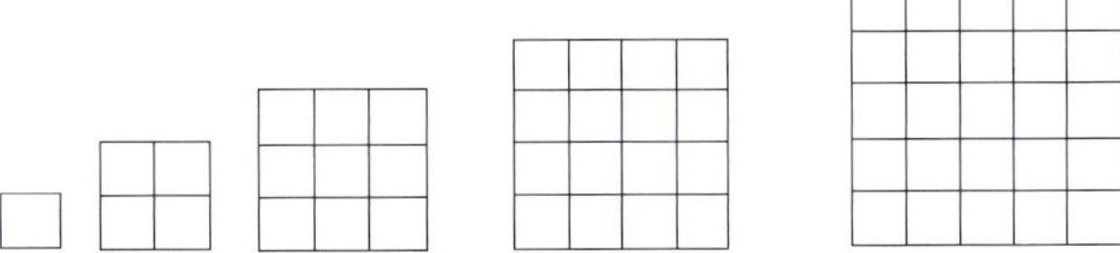

1 × 1 squares	1	4			
2 × 2 squares	0	1			
3 × 3 squares	0	0			
4 × 4 squares	0	0			
5 × 5 squares	0	0			

5 Investigate the number of cubes in each shape. Remember to include different sized cubes. Copy and fill in the table. Look for patterns and see if you can predict the number of cubes in the next shape of the sequence.

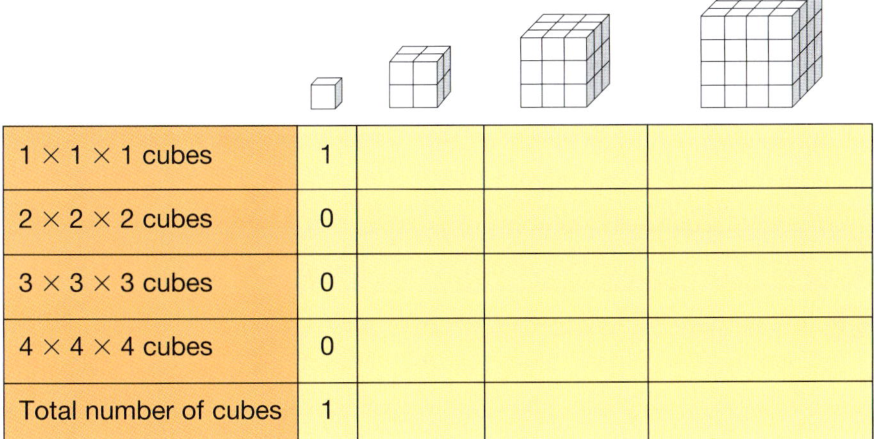

1 × 1 × 1 cubes	1			
2 × 2 × 2 cubes	0			
3 × 3 × 3 cubes	0			
4 × 4 × 4 cubes	0			
Total number of cubes	1			

6 Investigate the total number of triangles in this design.

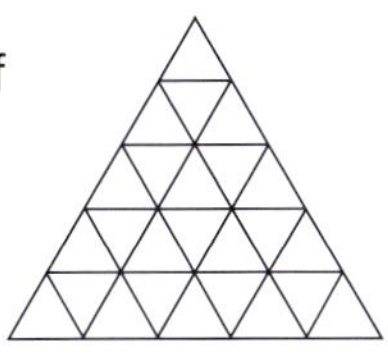

Try it yourself!

Is it possible to have a triangle with two obtuse angles? Explain your answer.

How did I do?

I can investigate and solve shape and space problems. ✔

23: Statistics

You will revise:

- what an 'average' is
- how to find different types of average.

Get started

Averages are used to represent a middle or typical value in a set of numbers. There are three types of average: mean, median and mode.

- To find the **mode**, look for the most popular, or frequent, value or values in the list or table.
- To find the **median**, put all the values in order and then find the middle value. If there are two middle values then the median is the number halfway between them.
- To find the **mean**, find the total of all the values and then divide this by the number of values.
- To find the mean when the data is in a table, multiply each value by the frequency and find the total. Then divide by the total frequency. For example:

Score (s)	Frequency (f)	$s \times f$
4	1	4
5	2	10
6	2	12
7	4	28
Totals	**9**	**54**

$54 \div 9 = 6$, so the mean is **6**.

Practice

1 Find the mode, median and mean of this set of data.

Dimitri's maths test scores (out of 10): 8 9 5 8 10

Challenge

2 Find the mode, median and mean of each set of data.

a 5 7 6 5 4 8 0 4 7 9 5 8 10

b 2 3 5 2 4 7 8 8 3 7 3 5

c 15 12 14 17 14 18 19 14 25 33

3 Copy and complete the table to find the mean of this set of data. You may use a calculator.

Score (s)	Frequency (f)	$s \times f$
0	7	
1	5	
2	6	
3	2	
Totals		

Mean = ____

4 Copy and complete the table to find the mean of this set of data. You may use a calculator.

Score (s)	Frequency (f)	$s \times f$
2	3	
3	6	
4	2	
5	2	
6	5	
Totals		

Mean = ____

5 Copy and complete the table to find the mean of this set of data. Then state the mode. You may use a calculator.

Score (s)	Frequency (f)	$s \times f$
4	3	
5	7	
6	4	
7	1	
8	9	
9	6	
Totals		

Mean = ____ Mode = ____

Try it yourself!

Write five numbers that have a mean of 6, a mode of 5 and a median of 5.

How did I do?

✔

I know what an average represents. ☐

I can find the mode, median and mean of a set of data. ☐

24: Graphs and charts

You will revise:

- how to construct a grouped frequency table
- how to draw and interpret bar charts and frequency diagrams.

Get started

When organising numerical information it is sometimes better to group the data to make it more meaningful and manageable. This **frequency table**, that represents the amount of money a group of children raised for charity, shows the data grouped into **equal class intervals**.

Amount of money raised to the nearest pound (£)	Frequency
10–14	2
15–19	6
20–24	6
25–29	4
30–34	2

Practice

1. This data shows the number of hours of TV watched by 24 pupils during one week:

   16, 4, 8, 17, 22, 37, 36, 25, 24, 9, 37, 44, 48, 35, 25, 27, 11, 23, 27, 36, 41, 39, 36, 20

   Copy and complete the frequency table for the data.

Number of hours	Tally	Frequency
0–9		
10–		

Challenge

2 This data shows the age (in years) of 40 people at a cinema.

47, 12, 11, 15, 19, 32, 37, 45, 52, 52,
15, 19, 14, 25, 27, 46, 74, 62, 11, 55,
42, 38, 38, 15, 17, 34, 32, 27, 24, 26,
37, 57, 48, 81, 42, 17, 64, 47, 11, 34

a Copy and complete the frequency table for the data.

Age (in years)	Tally	Frequency
0–19		
20–		

b Now show the data in a bar chart/frequency diagram. Use graph paper or squared paper. Make sure you label the axes and give the chart a title.

3 Use your bar chart to help you answer these questions.

a How many people at the cinema were aged between 20 and 39?

b How many more people were aged between 40 and 59 than between 60 and 79?

c How many more people were under 20 than were over 79?

d What is the modal age group?

e Is it true or false to say that more than half of the people at the cinema were under 40?

f Is it true or false to say that less than 5% of the people at the cinema were 80 or over?

4 Suggest who to ask, how many to ask, where and when a sample might be taken to collect data to help you answer this question:

Can taller people hold their breath longer than shorter people?

How did I do?

I can construct a grouped frequency table. ☐

I can draw and interpret bar charts and frequency diagrams. ☐

25: Probability

You will revise:

- how to find probabilities using equally likely outcomes.

Get started

Probability is about the chance, or likelihood, of something happening. The probability of something happening can be measured in several ways:

- seeing how often it has happened before
- by doing an experiment
- using equally likely outcomes.

To find a probability using equally likely outcomes you can use this formula:

$$\text{Probability } (P) = \frac{\text{the number of things you want}}{\text{the number of equally likely outcomes}}$$

Practice

1 Use equally likely outcomes to write the probabilities of these events as fractions.

- **a** Tossing a coin to land on heads.
- **b** Rolling a number 3 on a normal dice.
- **c** Choosing at random a day of the week starting with the letter S.

Challenge

2 Use equally likely outcomes to write the probabilities of these events as fractions.

- **a** Choosing at random a vowel from the alphabet.
- **b** Choosing at random an ace from a pack of cards.
- **c** Choosing at random a diamond from a pack of cards.
- **d** Rolling an even number on a normal dice.
- **e** Rolling a multiple of 3 on a normal dice.
- **f** Rolling a number greater than 6 on a normal dice.

3. One of these cards is picked at random.

0 1 2 3 4 5 6 7 8 9

What is the probability that it will:

a be a 4?

b not be a 4?

c be a number greater than 5?

d not be a number greater than 5?

e be a square number?

f not be a square number?

g be a prime number?

h not be a prime number?

4. Kate has 8 cards, numbered 1 to 8. She picks one at random. Mark on a 0–1 probability scale the probability that the number is greater than 5.

5. There are 8 teams left in the quarter finals of the cup. The names are written onto cards and put into a bag. They will be picked at random.

Arsenal	Liverpool	Derby County	Manchester United
Leeds United	Leicester City	Southampton	Oxford United

Write the probability, as a fraction in its simplest form, of the first club drawn from the bag:

a being Arsenal

b beginning with a vowel

c beginning with an 'L'

d ending with a 'd'

e containing a 'p'

f containing an 'e'

g consisting of two words

h having an odd number of letters

i containing 11 letters

j containing 12 letters

k beginning and ending with the same letter

l containing two consecutive letters in the same sequence as they appear in the alphabet, e.g. ab.

6. A spinner is made from a regular dodecagon (12 sides). The probability of spinning each colour is:

$\frac{1}{4}$ red $\frac{1}{3}$ yellow $\frac{1}{6}$ green $\frac{1}{12}$ blue $\frac{2}{12}$ pink

How many sections are shaded for each colour?

How did I do?

	✔
I can find probabilities using equally likely outcomes.	☐

Answers

1 Place value and decimals

1 a 6241 b 31 024
c 1 711 632 d 2 309 080
e 62.096

2 a 400 000 b 0.008 or $\frac{8}{1000}$
c 0.6 or $\frac{6}{10}$ d 8 000 000
e 800 f 4000
g 0.01 or $\frac{1}{100}$

3 a 10 000 + 7000 + 70 + 0.2
b 8000 + 400 + 80 + 1 + 0.3
c 2 + 0.7 + 0.05 + 0.008
d 1 000 000 + 20 000 + 3000 + 800 + 50 + 3 + 0.9
e 300 000 + 3000 + 40 + 2 + 0.5 + 0.03 + 0.007

4 a subtract 0.001 b add 1
c subtract 10 d add 0.001
e add 0.1

5 a add 0.01 b add 0.001
c subtract 0.001 d subtract 0.001
e add 0.01 f add 0.001

6 a 652.9 − 256.9 = 396
b 59.26 − 2.659 = 56.601
c 259.6 − 96.25 = 163.35
d 9.265 − 9.256; 2.965 − 2.956 = 0.009
e 9652 − 2.569 = 9649.431

7 a 2.089, 2.09(0), 2.091, 2.092, 2.093
b 31.6(0), 31.59, 31.58, 31.57, 31.56
c 5.102, 5.112, 5.122, 5.132, 5.142

2 Fractions

1 Fractions equivalent to these are also acceptable.
a $\frac{4}{8}$ b $\frac{5}{9}$
c $\frac{15}{20}$ d $\frac{1}{6}$
e $\frac{3}{10}$ f $\frac{2}{5}$
g $\frac{6}{12}$

2 A, B, C, F, H

3 a $\frac{3}{5}$ b $\frac{5}{7}$
c $\frac{5}{9}$ d $\frac{1}{2}$
e $\frac{5}{12}$

4 a $\frac{6}{8} + \frac{1}{8} = \frac{7}{8}$
b $\frac{6}{10} + \frac{3}{10} = \frac{9}{10}$
c $\frac{7}{12} - \frac{2}{12} = \frac{5}{12}$
d $\frac{7}{9} - \frac{3}{9} = \frac{4}{9}$

5 $\frac{5}{9}$

6 Fractions equivalent to these are also acceptable.
a $\frac{3}{4}$ b $\frac{3}{8}$
c $\frac{4}{15}$ d $\frac{3}{6}$
e $\frac{7}{8}$ f $\frac{8}{10}$

7

$\frac{2}{5}$	$\frac{3}{10}$	$\frac{4}{5}$
$\frac{9}{10}$	$\frac{1}{2}$	$\frac{1}{10}$
$\frac{1}{5}$	$\frac{7}{10}$	$\frac{3}{5}$

8 $\frac{23}{60}$

3 Percentages

1 a 120, 60, 24, 2.4
b 80, 40, 16, 1.6

2 a £14 b 18 m
c £22 d 150 g
e 53 cm f 2.5 m

3 a 180, 72, 12, 4.8 b 48, 3.2, 24, 96

4 a £36 b 6 m
c £4 d 10 kg
e 54 cm f 66 m
g 63 mm h 18 cm
i 19 cm

5 a £21 b £1200
c 99 ounces

6 a 180, 90, 36, 18, 3.6, 1.8
b 216, 270, 54, 91.8, 39.6, 21.6
c 183.6, 126, 181.8, 57.6, 237.6, 55.8

7 a £397.10 b £794.20
c £1588.40

8 a 2% of 250, 4% of 250, 6% of 250
b For £250, even-numbered percentages are whole numbers of pounds.

4 Proportion

1 a 0.5, 50% b 0.1, 10%
c 0.3, 30% d 0.7, 70%
e 0.25, 25% f 0.75, 75%

2 a 0.75, 75% b 0.7, 70%
c 0.6, 60% d 0.4, 40%
e 0.08, 8% f 0.125, 12.5%

3 Fractions equivalent to these are also acceptable.
a 34%, $\frac{34}{100}$ b 98%, $\frac{98}{100}$
c 27%, $\frac{27}{100}$ d 3%, $\frac{3}{100}$
e 40%, $\frac{40}{100}$ f 70%, $\frac{70}{100}$

4 Fractions equivalent to these are also acceptable.
a $\frac{64}{100}$, 0.64 b $\frac{85}{100}$, 0.85
c $\frac{16}{100}$, 0.16 d $\frac{3}{100}$, 0.03
e $\frac{70}{100}$, 0.7 f $\frac{80}{100}$, 0.8

5 a $\frac{4}{8} = 0.5 = 50\%$ b $\frac{4}{10} = 0.4 = 40\%$
c $\frac{12}{16} = 0.75 = 75\%$

6 a $\frac{3}{10} = 0.3 = 30\%$ b $\frac{14}{16} = 0.875 = 87.5\%$
c $\frac{7}{20} = 0.35 = 35\%$

7 $0.65 = 65\% = \frac{13}{20}$

Try it yourself!
$\frac{3}{5} = 60\% = 0.6$

5 Ratio

1 a 3 : 4 b 1 : 2
c 9 : 1 d 2 : 3
e 3 : 4 f 2 : 5
g 6 : 4 : 3 h 3 : 6 : 2

2 a 1 : 5 b 1 : 6
c 5 : 6 d 1 : 5 : 6

3 £18, £45

4 £21, £28

5 £56, £16

6 £8, £16, £64

7 £36, £24, £60

8 £70, £140, £350

9 40°, 100°, 40°; isosceles

10 120°, 30°, 120°, 90°; right-angled kite

11 1 : 3

12 a 0 : 6, 1 : 5, 2 : 4, 3 : 3, 4 : 2, 5 : 1, 6 : 0
b 0 : 8, 1 : 7, 2 : 6, 3 : 5, 4 : 4, 5 : 3, 6 : 2, 7 : 1, 8 : 0
c 0 : 9, 1 : 8, 2 : 7, 3 : 6, 4 : 5, 5 : 4, 6 : 3, 7 : 2, 8 : 1, 9 : 0
d 0 : 12, 1 : 11, 2 : 10, 3 : 9, 4 : 8, 5 : 7, 6 : 6, 7 : 5, 8 : 4, 9 : 3, 10 : 2, 11 : 1, 12 : 0
e 4 : 2, 6 : 3, 8 : 4
f 2 : 6, 3 : 9
g 4 : 2, 5 : 3, 7 : 5

6 Positive and negative numbers

1 a 3 b −5
c 4 d 5
e 4

2 a −5 b −3
c −12 d −7
e −9

3 a 4, −14, −4 b −9, 5, −5
c −4, −26, 4

4 a −12 b −11
c 7 d −14
e 4 f −25
g −7 h −32
i −17 j −45

5 a $-6 + 4 = -2$
b $-5 - 8 = -13$
c $5 - 9 = -4$
d $3 + 5 = 8$
e $-9 - 3 = -12$
f $15 + 11 = 26$
g $17 - 5 = 12$
h $-18 - 4 = -22$

6 a −2 b −4
c −2 d −5

7 a $-6 + 4$ b $8 + -6$
c $-11 - -9$ d $-9 - -11$

8 a

0	−1	4
5	1	−3
−2	3	2

b

−2	−3	2
3	−1	−5
−4	1	0

Try it yourself!

−4	−5	0
1	−3	−7
−6	−1	−2

7 Prime numbers, factors and multiples

1

×	1	2	3	4	5	6	7	8	9	10	11	12
3	3	6	9	12	15	18	21	24	27	30	33	36
4	4	8	12	16	20	24	28	32	36	40	44	48
5	5	10	15	20	25	30	35	40	45	50	55	60
6	6	12	18	24	30	36	42	48	54	60	66	72
7	7	14	21	28	35	42	49	56	63	70	77	84
8	8	16	24	32	40	48	56	64	72	80	88	96
9	9	18	27	36	45	54	63	72	81	90	99	108

2 a 12 b 21
c 56 d 18
e 40 f 18
g 36 h 60

3 a 1, 2, 4, 5, 10, 20
b 1, 2, 4, 8, 16
c 1, 5, 25,
d 1, 2, 3, 5, 6, 10, 15, 30
e 1, 2, 7, 14,
f 1, 3, 9, 27
g 1, 17
h 1, 5, 7, 35
i 1, 2, 3, 4, 6, 9, 12, 18, 36
j 1, 2, 4, 8, 16, 32

4 17

5 12, 18, 20, 28

6 a 7 b 4
c 1 d 10
e 16 f 5
g 6 h 2
i 3

7 4, 9, 16, 25. They are square numbers.

8 a 7 + 2 b 11 + 5
c 23 + 2 d 31 + 5
e 47 + 2 f 61 + 3
g 79 + 2 h 97 + 3

9 a 1 b 96
c 96

8 Understanding number

1 a 0 b 1
c 0 d 1
e 0 f 0
g 58 h 0
i 1 j 0
k 1 l 0

2 a false b true
c true d false
e true f true

3 a 33 b 30
c 8 d 12
e 13 f 2
g 10 h 36
i 15 j 13
k 10 l 3
m 36 n 30
o 19

4 A, B, E, F

5 a 264 + 264 + 264 b 7530 + 753
c 1034 ÷ 22 d 9320 − 932
e 2448 ÷ 72 f 3600 + 36
g 3670 h 87 400 − 874

6 a true b true
c true d false
e true f false

Try it yourself!

a $8 \times 4 + 2$ b $8 + 4 \times 2$
c $(8 + 2) \times 4$ d $(4 + 2) \times 8$

9 Calculations

1

0	7	2	36	30
54	24	3	60	8
0	81	10	63	5
54	36	3	2	72
10	3	2	63	49
42	28	5	56	0
64	56	32	72	2
48	3	5	10	1

2 a 49 b 5
c 81 d 7
e 100 f 25
g 2 h 36
i 3 j 144
k 1 l 121
m 4 n 44
o 2.5

3 a $0.3 \times 0.3 = 0.09$
b $0.4 \times 0.4 = 0.16$
c $0.5 \times 0.5 = 0.25$
d $0.6 \times 0.6 = 0.36$
e $0.7 \times 0.7 = 0.49$
f $0.8 \times 0.8 = 0.64$
g $0.9 \times 0.9 = 0.81$
h $1.0 \times 1.0 = 1$
i $1.1 \times 1.1 = 1.21$
j $1.2 \times 1.2 = 1.44$

4 a 64p b 86p
c £8.80 d £73.50
e £8.60

5 a 0.35 b 45
c 7.5 d 55
e 1.5 f 2.5
g 35 h 0.85
i 3.7 j 0.2
k 0.95 l 41
m 0.36 n 44
o 7.3

6 a 1042 b 1167
c 1251 d 10.663
e 183 f 1279
g 9076 h 414.62
i 4224 j 11 424
k 848 l 37.434
m 213 n 207
o 61.6

Try it yourself!

The product of outer numbers is always 1 less than the square of the middle number.

With five consecutive numbers the product of outer numbers is always 4 less than the square of the middle number.

10 Problem solving (1)

1 a division b multiplication
c division d addition
e subtraction

2 a 144 b 6839
c 6 d 68
e 728 f 15p
g 34 h £5
i 27 j 14
k 19 l 44p
m 20p n £1.20
o 8 boxes; 7 full p 15
q 12 r £13
s 25% of £5 t £173 964
u £114.75

Try it yourself!

The footballer earns more.

The footballer earns £438 000 in a year.

The supermodel earns £404 712 in a year.

11 Simplifying expressions

1 a $5m + 3n$ b $7c + 3d$
c $13e + 3f$ d $6x + 7y$
e $9j + 6k$ f $9a + 3b + 4c$
g $4p + 9q + 3r$ h $11x + 8y + 8z$
i $3m + 9n + 8p$

2 a $6a + 10b + 13$ b $7a + 8b + 11$
c $9a + 11b + 7$ d $7a + 4b + 21$
e $11a + 6b + 17$

3

	$20n + 6m + 36$	
$13n + 3m + 15$	$7n + 3m + 21$	
$9n + 2m + 5$	$4n + m + 10$	$3n + 2m + 11$

4 a $a + 8b$ b $7e + 3f + 1$
c $2h + i + 2$ d $4t + 11u - 2$
e $6g - 5h + 4$ f $-p + 11q - 3$
g $3x + 3y - 4$ h $-m - 3n + 13$

5 a $4a + 2b + 9$ and $5b - 3a + 3$
b $6a - b + 4$ and $3a - 5b - 2$
c $3a + 6b - 9$ and $-a - b + 9$
d $3a - 5b - 2$ and $3b - 2a$

Try it yourself!

Check your expressions by simplifying them. Do you get the expression $5x + 2y - 1$ each time?

12 Linear equations

1 a $n \times 25 = 175, n = 7$
b $n \div 6 = 12, n = 72$
c $n - 12 = 79, n = 91$
d $n + 36 = 78, n = 42$
e $20 - n = 4, n = 16$

2 a $2n + 5 = 75, n = 35$
b $3n + 1 = 19, n = 6$
c $5n - 1 = 39, n = 8$
d $8n - 7 = 57, n = 8$

3 a $a = 5$ b $y = 5$
c $f = 4$ d $p = 5$
e $d = 7$ f $c = 8$
g $b = 10$ h $e = 5$
i $a = 8$ j $y = 3$
k $f = 4$ l $p = 3$
m $d = 10$ n $c = 8$
o $b = 11$

4 $n = 25$; other angles: 35°, 45°

5 a $x = 14$ b $x = 92$

Try it yourself!

£18

13 Formulae and substituting

1 a £6 b £8
c £16 d £22
e £18 f £30

2 a £14 b £17
c £26 d £23
e £20 f £35
g £29 h £41

3 a 19 b 25
c 61

4 a 28 b 34
c 54 d 0

5 a $P \approx 14$ b $P \approx 21$
c $P \approx 42$ d $P \approx 49$
e $P \approx 56$ f $P \approx 77$
g $P \approx 140$ h $P \approx 175$
i $P \approx 84$

6 a 19 b 18
c 24 d 26
e 35

7 a F, $W = 3(7 - n)$
b G, $W = 2(n + 4)$
c C, $W = 5n - 3$
d E, $W = n^2$

8 $P = 3N + 1$

14 Sequences

1 a 9, 11, 13, 15, 17, 19, 21, 23
b 74, 69, 64, 59, 54, 49, 44, 39
c 127, 137, 147, 157, 167, 177, 187, 197
d 1, 2, 4, 8, 16, 32, 64, 128
e 512, 256, 128, 64, 32, 16, 8, 4

2 a First term 5, increasing by 3.
b First term 77, decreasing by 5.
c First term 10, decreasing by 2.5.
d First term 0.8, decreasing by 0.2.

3 a 0, 0.25, 0.5, 0.75, 1, 1.25, 1.5, 1.75
b 17.5, 17, 16.5, 16, 15.5, 15, 14.5, 14
c 12.7, 12.8, 12.9, 13, 13.1, 13.2, 13.3, 13.4
d 6.25, 6.15, 6.05, 5.95, 5.85, 5.75, 5.65, 5.55
e 8.4, 8.9, 9.4, 9.9, 10.4, 10.9, 11.4, 11.9

4 a 7, 13, 19, 25, 31
b 2, 6, 10, 14, 18

5 a First term is 7, each term increases by 7. Multiply the position number by 7.
b First term is 6, each term increases by 5. Multiply the position number by 5 and add 1.

6 a Any sequences that meet the criteria, such as 5, 10, 15, 20, 25, 30, . . .
First term is 5, each term increases by 5. Multiply the position number by 5.
b Any sequences that meet the criteria, such as 2, 4, 6, 8, 10, 12, . . .
First term is 2, each term increases by 2. Multiply the position number by 2.
c Any sequences that meet the criteria, such as 3, 13, 23, 33, 43, . . .
First term is 3, each term increases by 10. Multiply the position number by 10 and subtract 7.

15 Problem solving (2)

1 a CD = $3x$ b EF = $3x + 1$
c 15 cm d 22 cm

2 a $x = 3d$ b $P = 9d$
c $x = 12$ cm d $P = 36$ cm
e $d = 10$ cm

3 a AC = $2r$ b AB = $d + r$
c $P = 4(d + r)$ d Area = $(d + r)^2$

4 a 20 cm b 14.1 cm
c 56.4 cm d 198.81 cm^2

5 Length = 16 cm, width = 8 cm

16 Angles

1 $a = 138°$, $b = 65°$, $c = 80°$, $d = 22°$, $e = 95°$

2 $a = 51°$, $b = 36°$, $c = 119°$

3 $d = 82°$, $e = 36°$, $f = 144°$

4 $g = 50°$, $h = 68°$, $i = 2°$, $j = 110°$, $k = 68°$

5 $a = 50°$, $b = 95°$, $c = 35°$

6 a 145° b 130°
c 85°
They are the same.

Try it yourself!

124°, 56°, 124°

Using knowledge that angles on a straight line add up to 180° and 180° − 56° = 124°.

17 Coordinates

1 A (−2, 3), B (0, −4), C (−4, −1), D (4, −1)

2

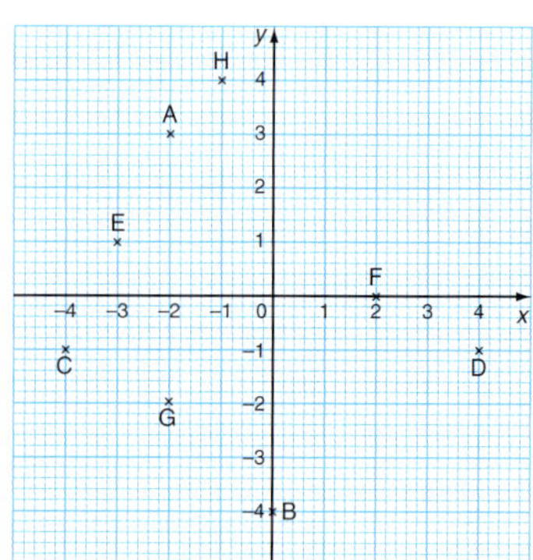

3 a (−1, 0) b (3, −2)
c (0, −3)

4 (5, −3)

5 (−1, −6)

6 (3, 0) (0, 3)

7 (2, 0) (0, −2)

8 (−1, −4) (−3, −2)

9 F, (−4, −2)

10 F, (−3, −4)

Try it yourself!
3

18 Constructing triangles

1 a 7 cm b 32°
c 4.5 cm

2 4.5 cm

3 1.7 cm

4 a 32° b 6.1 cm
c 61°

5 a 69° b 6.9 cm
c 5.2 cm

6 a 58° b 7.7 cm
c 3.2 cm

7 Triangle 1: right-angled scalene
Triangle 2: scalene
Triangle 3: obtuse isosceles

19 Perimeter and area

1 20 cm, 21 cm^2

2 23 cm, 30 cm^2

3 a 40 cm, 79 cm^2
b 38 cm, 76 cm^2
c 40 cm, 88 cm^2

4 a 28 cm, 39 cm^2
b 40 cm, 85 cm^2
c 42 cm, 96 cm^2

5 a 40 cm, 64 cm^2
b 44 cm, 81 cm^2
c 50 cm, 90 cm^2

Try it yourself!
28 cm

20 Surface area

1 184 cm^2

2 142 cm^2

3 280 cm^2

4 a 358 cm^2 b 228 cm^2
c 112 cm^2 d 474 cm^2

5 5 cm

21 Measurement

1 a 300 b 3
c 6 d 47
e 9 f 20
g 500 h 7000
i 600 j 4000
k 8 l 70 000

2 a 1 b 7
c 4.5 d 8000
e 3500 f 5700
g 1500 h 2.5
i 16 800

3 a 370 b 1.28
c 6.7 d 47.3
e 0.986 f 2.38
g 4.902 h 0.354
i 78

4 a 1.2 b 1.64
c 4.362 d 0.866
e 3500 f 5330
g 1584 h 1.647
i 16 670

5 a 0.15 b 1
c 0.025 d 0.362
e 0.013 87 f 560
g 1.56 h 0.089
i 5.66 j 8.092
k 0.008 67 l 81 900

6 a false b true
c false d true
e true f false
g true h false

7 Equivalent facts such as: 0.64 m = 640 mm, 0.000 46 km = 46 cm

22 Problem solving (3)

1 14

2 13

3 a 3 b 4
c 1, 2, 4, 7, 11, 16, 22

4

1 × 1 squares	1	4	9	16	25
2 × 2 squares	0	1	4	9	16
3 × 3 squares	0	0	1	4	9
4 × 4 squares	0	0	0	1	4
5 × 5 squares	0	0	0	0	2

5

1 × 1 × 1 cubes	1	8	27	64
2 × 2 × 2 cubes	0	1	8	27
3 × 3 × 3 cubes	0	0	1	8
4 × 4 × 4 cubes	0	0	0	1
Total number of cubes	1	9	36	100

6 There are 48 triangles in the pattern.
25 + 13 + 6 + 3 + 1 = 48

Try it yourself!
No, it is impossible because the angles inside a triangle add to 180°. If there were two obtuse angles (between 90° and 180°), then the angles would have a sum greater than 180°.

23 Statistics

1 8, 8, 8

2 a 5, 6, 6 b 3, 4.5, 4.7
c 14, 16, 18.1

3 1.15

4 4

5 6.8, 8

Try it yourself!
Example answer: 3, 5, 5, 8, 9

24 Graphs and charts

1

Number of hours	Frequency
0–9	3
10–19	3
20–29	8
30–39	7
40–49	3

2 a

Age (in years)	Frequency
0–19	12
20–39	13
40–59	11
60–79	3
80–99	1

b Bar chart showing age of people at a cinema.

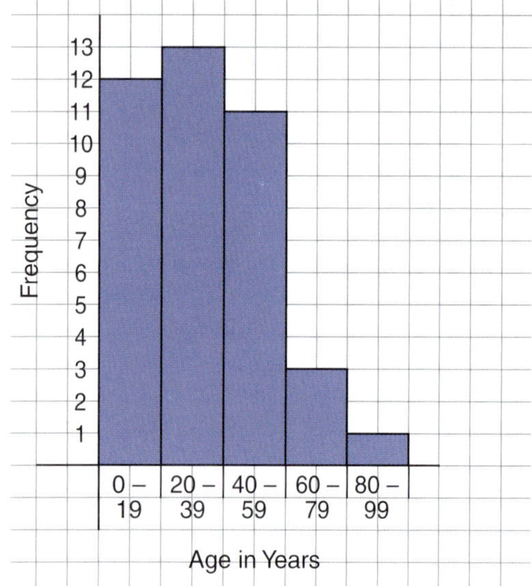

3 **a** 13 **b** 8
c 11 **d** 20–39
e true **f** true

4 Any sensible answer.

25 Probability

1 **a** $\frac{1}{2}$ **b** $\frac{1}{6}$
c $\frac{2}{7}$

2 Fractions equivalent to these are also acceptable.
a $\frac{5}{26}$ **b** $\frac{1}{13}$ or $\frac{4}{52}$
c $\frac{1}{4}$ or $\frac{13}{52}$ **d** $\frac{3}{6}$ or $\frac{1}{2}$
e $\frac{2}{6}$ or $\frac{1}{3}$ **f** 0

3 Fractions equivalent to these are also acceptable.
a $\frac{1}{10}$ **b** $\frac{9}{10}$
c $\frac{4}{10}$ **d** $\frac{6}{10}$
e $\frac{3}{10}$ **f** $\frac{7}{10}$
g $\frac{4}{10}$ **h** $\frac{6}{10}$

4 $\frac{3}{8}$ marked on a 0–1 probability scale, e.g. 3 cm from 0 mark on an 8 cm-long scale

5 **a** $\frac{1}{8}$ **b** $\frac{1}{4}$
c $\frac{3}{8}$ **d** $\frac{3}{8}$
e $\frac{1}{4}$ **f** $\frac{7}{8}$
g $\frac{5}{8}$ **h** $\frac{3}{4}$
i $\frac{3}{8}$ **j** $\frac{1}{8}$
k $\frac{1}{8}$ **l** $\frac{1}{2}$

6 3, 4, 2, 1, 2

Note to parents

The *Challenge Maths* series is designed to challenge and extend children aged 11–14 in the key maths topics in the curriculum at Key Stage 3. There are three books in the series, one for each year group, to cover the key mathematics topics specified in the Key Stage 3 National Strategy. The *Challenge Maths* books involve the more complex aspects of maths in the curriculum and provide opportunities for children to be challenged and extended in their understanding.

The books are designed to be used by children throughout the year. Each double-page spread provides information about the nature of the topic, the key aspects that children are expected to master, and provides opportunities for them to practise and test their own understanding.

By working through the *Challenge Maths* book, your child will encounter the more difficult mathematics concepts appropriate for that year group and be encouraged to solve problems and puzzles requiring an advanced level of mathematical thinking.

The maths curriculum at KS3 and the National Tests

The Key Stage 3 Strategy is designed to make the most of the time between primary school and GCSEs. It provides training for teachers, materials for pupils and advice for everyone involved in making the classroom experience as effective as possible. The Strategy provides a framework for teaching mathematics in Years 7, 8 and 9, identifying the aspects of maths to be taught and the expectations for pupils. The main strands of learning at Key Stage 3 are as follows.

- Using and applying mathematics to solve problems.
- Numbers and the number system.
- Calculations.
- Algebra.
- Shape, space and measures.
- Handling data.

Children at Key Stage 3 who attend state schools in England sit National Tests (also known as SATs) at the age of 14. Children in Wales may take the same tests at 14. All children may also sit optional tests aged 12 and 13 – many schools have chosen to adopt these tests. The results are used by the school to assess each child's level of knowledge and progress in maths, English and science. They also provide guidance for the child's next teacher when he or she is planning the coming year.

The *Challenge* series provides opportunities for children to prepare for these tests, by ensuring that they are challenged in the more complex topics for their particular year group. It is important that this is not a last-minute activity, but forms part of the on-going revision work throughout the year. The children who succeed in maths are those who evaluate their own understanding of each topic as they encounter it and take steps to improve areas of difficulty by further study. The *Challenge* series provides a wide range of opportunities for children to be stretched and to meet the more difficult mathematical problems that they may face in the National Tests.

Levels of attainment

Teachers gain information about your child's progress through testing and ongoing teacher assessment. You will be informed each year of your child's level of attainment. Each level is a measure that teachers use to check how much your child knows, understands and can do. National expectations are that by the end of Key Stage 1 pupils achieve at least level 2, by the end of Key Stage 2 level 4 and above, and by the end of Key Stage 3 level 5 and above.

The materials in this book are designed to help extend children working at level 5 or above.

How to use this book

Encourage your child to work through the topics in this book and test their understanding by answering the questions and solving the problems and puzzles. It is not necessary to work through the topics in the order that they are given.

Throughout the book are 'Try it yourself!' puzzles which encourage your child to develop more effective thinking skills and provide more complex situations for children to challenge themselves with. These can be tackled independently of the rest of the page and can serve as a revision question when a topic is revisited.

What can parents do to help?

Learning, and especially revision, is best if active. The more effective practice in a topic a child experiences the more confident he or she will become. The more confident a child is, the more ready they are for challenges and extension work, which leads to greater achievement.

Once a child thinks they have mastered a topic it can help if you offer to be the pupil! Can they teach it to you? If they can teach you something, they really know and understand it! Explaining something to someone else is one of the best ways of consolidating learning. This approach also shows that you are interested in the topics they are learning and are acknowledging and celebrating their progress.

What next?

Once children have worked through the *Challenge* book for their year group and are confident with all the topics, they can prepare for the National Tests using the *WHS National Tests Practice Papers*. These contain Practice tests to be taken under examination conditions and can help you to assess the level at which your child is working.